Journey Back to You

A guide to meeting your authentic self

Danielle McCarron

The content of this book is for general informational purposes only. It is not meant to be used, nor should it be used, to diagnose or treat any medical condition or to replace the services of your physician or other healthcare provider. The advice and strategies contained in the book may not be suitable for all readers. Please consult your healthcare provider with any questions that you may have about your own medical situation. Neither the author, publisher, IIN nor any of their employees or representatives guarantee the accuracy of information in this book or its usefulness to a particular reader, nor are they responsible for any damage or negative consequence that may result from any treatment, action taken or inaction by any person reading or following the information in this book.

You've always had the power my dear, you just had to learn it for yourself.

– The Wizard of Oz

Thank you to everyone who believed in me until I could believe in myself.

To everyone who feels they cannot believe in themselves yet - I will believe in you until you do.

<u>The Journey</u>

What It's All About

*It is my wholehearted belief that all of our struggles, all of our pain,
addiction and suffering – that the crisis of the world – is due to a
disconnect from our authentic selves.*
- *Danielle McCarron*

It was July 3rd, 2014. I was looking in the mirror for the first time in what felt like years. I was unrecognizable. I had embarrassed myself and my family, yet again. I had made promises I immediately broke, yet again. I couldn't do *anything* without having a panic attack. I was drunk, 24/7. The reflection staring back at me wasn't me at all – it looked like someone else entirely. I looked like I was possessed. How had I become this person?

After washing my face, I somehow mustered up the courage to look at myself again – really look at myself. I slowly made eye contact with my reflection, something I don't ever remember doing before. I was so ashamed of my behaviour I couldn't really look at myself except to drunkenly put make-up on. When the contact was made, I saw something I hadn't seen in so, so long. Through the possession of my addiction, and through the disgrace and shame, I saw a glimmer of hope. For just a split second, I knew I was still there. Somewhere in this mess of a person I had become, I could see who I really was underneath it all. A moment later I called a friend who was in recovery and reached out for help. I had just turned 24 years old, and I had hit my rock bottom.

From a great family, a beautiful home in a neighbourhood referred to as "Pleasantville" in Toronto, I wasn't the person who was supposed to become an alcoholic. I grew up in a lovely home, I was succeeding at law school and I appeared to be really doing well in life. However, inside I was an absolute fucking wreck. I had been that way for as long as I could remember. How had I become this person? I felt completely disconnected from myself.

And that's where my journey of self-discovery and healing really began, with what felt like the end. I genuinely believed my life was over. How could I possibly live without alcohol? The real problem was that I knew I was going to die pretty soon if I kept on down this path. I also knew that I couldn't keep living this way. There was nothing left for me in the bottle. That's where so many journeys start, and mine is no exception. It all started from the bottom. I was terrified, more vulnerable than I had ever been, and more willing to change than ever before. I had to hit the bottom to be able to admit defeat and look for another way of living. I had to change everything in my life. This has taken time, intention and a lot of hard work. What came out of this process was an ability to live from a place of honesty and truth. I am living my life as I really am.

The thing is, as soon as I put down the booze, I started to enjoy my life again. I quickly started to feel this passion and connection within me that I didn't know I had. I became curious about recovery, about how to heal myself and about how to really live the best life I could. I am not sure why, but I started to believe the things that I was hearing, from people who had been in my shoes. I gained hope and faith through their stories, through their honesty and their vulnerability. I started to put myself back together, and I was actually enjoying the journey.

In attempting to stay sober, I learned that my addiction wasn't the problem – my addiction was an attempt to solve the problem.

I had been using this solution for years and it was no longer working for me. It was a solution to pain, dissatisfaction, inherent unworthiness and a need to escape. It was a solution to a problem with life that I didn't know I had. What I soon discovered was that this came from a complete disconnect to my authentic self, to who I truly was. I had been running my life from pieces of me that weren't really me, aiming for goals that weren't mine, being in relationships that didn't serve me, escaping reality as often as I could. I was trying desperately to connect to something outside of myself because I didn't know how to get what I really needed, and I didn't know how to get what I really needed because I didn't know *what* I needed! I didn't have access to who I really was, so how could I possibly know what I needed?

I had spent so much of my life concerned with how I looked, what other people thought of me and trying to meet the expectations of others that had absolutely nothing to do with me. I was operating from years and years of intergenerational conditioning that was not really my true self. This all led to an entirely severed relationship with who I really am, and a disease that would ultimately kill me if I did not look at the underlying issues. These underlying issues are what I will be addressing throughout this book. If the language I am using right now seems unclear or confusing – it will clear up.

Anger, resentment, fear, shame, lies, betrayal, blame, guilt, unworthiness – these were the defaults of how I was living my life.

The beauty of it all? I would never have been able to become the person I am today without this struggle. I would never have been willing to change myself if I had not self-destructed entirely.

None of this is to say that I cannot still be a walking train wreck. I operate consistently from old conditioning and fear. I have accepted that this will be a life-long journey of removing layers of programming – of stuff that isn't mine. As soon as I feel some relief as one area of my life heals and grows, another area that needs healing pops up. This is the natural ebb and flow of life, and it can be an insane rollercoaster with super highs and lows. But, it can also be really incredible, exciting and rewarding.

I will never be perfect and thank God for that. It actually excites me now that this is a life-long process, as each layer that is removed brings me closer and closer to my authentic self and makes this one life an even deeper and more profound experience. I will be vulnerable and I will admit when I am wrong – which is often – and I will align myself with my authenticity and faith every day to be the best version of myself that I can be. Some days that person is super outgoing, optimistic, positive and full of faith and love. Sometimes, that person is a raging bitch who needs to avoid people because she feels like she is going to tear someone apart. Sometimes, she is calm and serene, and sometimes she needs a swift kick in the butt. Sometimes, that person is really hard-working and dedicated, and sometimes she can be a fairly ridiculous human being. The thing is, I know now that I am always doing the best I can, in each and every moment.

What I came to understand was that through a profound healing journey, I can not only learn who I really am and what I really need, but I can trust wholeheartedly in those needs and desires. That person is my authentic self. That person is entirely good, beautiful and whole on her own. But somewhere along the line, I wasn't able to access her anymore. This entire journey has led me back to her, to who I really am. Sometimes, I lose her by not acknowledging her enough. But now I have the tools to get back in touch with my truth and live as I am meant to live.

A disconnect from our authentic selves is the root of all the fear, hatred, discontent and addiction happening in the world today. It is the undercurrent of intolerance and the deep fears we all have. We need to see others as separate from us because we aren't in touch with who we are. It scares us when others are different. This is the root of why we exist *through* life but don't really live it. This book is designed to take you through the processes I have been through to access my authentic self and start living a life that is true to me. I believe that if we live in a world where every person is living in their truth, we will know peace. This is my way of making a difference.

Together we will look at how to become aware of what the blocks are, and how to release fear, shame and guilt. How to have authentic relationships and fulfil our need for true, meaningful connection. How to live a healthy life – mind, body, spirit. How to embrace who we really are and let go of the fear of living our best lives.

What I am hoping to share with you is how this all happened for me and how I was able to begin the process of accessing my authentic self. I feel called to share with you what my journey has looked like in order to help others through my experience. I have undergone a profound transformation and a removal of layers that I had built up over time in order to access my truth. I hope that by sharing my experience, strength and hope, I can help others transform their lives as I have learned to transform my own. I have found freedom through this process and it feels like my duty and responsibility to share the tools that have led to that freedom with you. This book is meant to act as a guide to help you let go of old conditioning – to become who you are meant to be. I believe that every person has the ability to heal within them. I am simply here to provide you with some tools to help you access your own resources. I hope that by sharing my truth with you, it will help you find the faith in something bigger, but mostly, to know wholeheartedly that you are perfect the way you are. The world needs you, and I have faith you can find yourself through this process the way I have.

How the Book is Laid Out

The book is simple and concise and includes my interpretation of learning from the Transformational Arts College of Spiritual and Holistic Training in Toronto, the Institute for Integrative Nutrition, 12-step recovery programs, books, lectures, research, spiritual teachers and a passion for healing and growth. I have links to all of these sources on my website. For further information on each, please go to daniellemccarron.com.

I will take you on a journey through the five layers which are blocking you from living in authenticity. The layers are:

1. Shame and Shadow
2. Core Beliefs
3. False Selves
4. Defences
5. Addiction

To start us off, I'll show you what my journey has looked like. Then, we will look at our authentic self and discuss the initial disconnects that block us from our authenticity. I am beginning with the authentic self so you can have an idea of where the freedom lies. The layers will be discussed in terms of initial disconnects from our authentic self and how each layer has developed on top of another. Then, we will look at how we have built layers on top of who we really are. These layers are our personalities, our defences, our addictions, our core beliefs and our shame. Each layer builds upon itself until we are completely disconnected from who we really are. As you will see, the program goes through the layers that are blocking us from our essence – from our true authenticity. Each layer is explained using my experiences of moving through them; some are old blocks that I have already moved through and some I am still working on uncovering.

For every layer, a similar format is followed. The first chapter of the book explains each of these layers in more detail and how each chapter is uniquely tailored to help best serve you in moving through your blocks. Each layer will follow the process of what I like to call "getting curious" and then living in our new-found freedom. It will always follow the same steps:

1. Awareness
2. Acceptance
3. Action (Surrender)
4. Healing

These are the four steps of transformation and are explained in Chapter 3. Chapter 11 is also dedicated to transformation and healing.

This is the start of your journey into a beautifully authentic life. It is a process, and this program is meant as a design for living. It is to help you design a life that you love and to guide you in discovering who you really are and what your true desires are. Everyone will need to start at different points. Do the practices that resonate with you. Try the ones that scare you. Be gentle with yourself. Come back through each chapter as you are ready. There will be pieces that are revealed to you right away, then, maybe months or years from now, something else from the book will resonate with you in a different way.

Remember that it is okay to feel; feelings won't kill you and will be the entry point to healing pain. Suppressing how we are feeling and not honouring where we are at can be more painful than anything. This can be a beautiful and miraculous journey but looking at yourself can also be pretty icky at times. Be honest with yourself, trust your gut and let it guide you on this journey.

I have been as honest as I can throughout this entire book. I am here to let you know that you are never alone, that I have felt the way you are feeling, and I have transformed my life. I do share the good parts of moving through the pain, as well as the freedom I feel in releasing each layer, to provide hope that there is joy and there is freedom on the other side. If I can leave you with one thing, right from the get-go, it is that I would not be going through this journey and process still if it hadn't opened me up to so much laughter, fun and true connections in my life. By becoming who I really am, I have been able to design a life that I love, a life that really works for me, and I have found so much joy through it all.

Introduction
My Story

She was never afraid to wear a smile, for happiness was her greatest

victory.

– Dane Thomas

I was a party girl. The friend you grabbed for a good time. I was a hell of a lot of fun. I encouraged everyone around me to get obliterated, "let go" and have a good time. Every time I drank, I would inevitably be dancing on something – a table, the bar, a chair – anything. And, I would definitely be encouraging others to do the same. I had fun for a long time. I was a good student, so it was hard for anyone to be overly concerned about my drinking as my grades didn't reflect those of someone with a "problem," but I was actually on the verge of full-blown alcoholism.

I remember the morning I felt like I had crossed the line. I was in my last year of undergrad, and all of our friends typically got together for brunch (at 3 p.m.) after a solid night out to rehash the previous evening and hang out. I loved a good drink the next day to take the edge off, but it always seemed like harmless fun and everyone else was doing it. This particular day, my friends were all hanging out and I remember feeling that not drinking was no longer an option. I was a bit shaky and my anxiety was through

1

the roof. I felt like I was going to die. Not exaggerating, I genuinely thought I might die if I didn't get another drink in me. So, I ordered a glass of wine at breakfast when nobody else was drinking. I always played it off like I was just SO much fun that it wasn't an issue, and at that point, most people didn't think anything of it. But, the awareness that this might not be a casual thing anymore began to creep in.

I was a bit freaked out but brushed it off and carried on. From that point, I felt as though I had found the magic elixir to life. I could be numb most of the time, not feel the pain and anxiety, have fun and keep killing it at school. Score. Life's problems seemed to be solved.

I had been disconnected from myself for quite some time now. As you continue through this book and go through the different layers, those parts will become clear. But, it all led to me being completely cut off from who I really was. The decisions I made weren't authentic decisions – I wasn't capable of them.

One of the biggest decisions I made in my life was to attend law school, except it didn't even really feel like a decision. I enjoyed a couple of law classes I took in my undergrad, really didn't want to have to enter the real world of looking for a job or not being supported by my parents, so I applied to law school. My heart was set on moving to London, mostly because I needed a change of scenery. In the recovery world, this is known as a "geographic cure," a.k.a. running away from your problems just to find out that YOU are the common denominator and that wherever you go, there you are. Anyway, I was accepted to the City University of London and I moved to the UK. Did I truly have any passion for learning law? No. Did I want the big office and paycheque and to be able to say that I was a law student and was someday going to be a lawyer? Hell, yeah. I felt that it was what I "should" be doing. I was smart and hard-working, so why not become a badass lawyer, right? Wrong. This was all ego, and clearly, I am not a lawyer.

My mom helped me move in September 2013. I had at least 12 meltdowns in the week she was there with me. I broke down over bedding, furniture, where we were going to eat, everything. I was terrified, and nothing felt right. That is because nothing was right. Everything in me, my authentic self, was screaming at me in every way it could get my attention to tell me that I was making the wrong decision. In hindsight, I knew the entire time that it was wrong for me. But, I had made the decision, so I had to stick it out, because a commitment is a commitment, and more importantly, what would people think if I didn't follow through? They would think I had failed, or I couldn't hack it, and it would validate my already very real fears that I wasn't good enough.

Of course, I couldn't change my reality. I remember the moment I admitted this out loud for the first time. I was smoking cigarettes out of my apartment window after having had a few glasses of wine (because I really deserved a break from studying) with my dear friend and roommate, Frances. She is one of the most important people in my life and really went through the trenches with me and my disease. I will be so forever grateful to her and her continued friendship. We always had these really incredible conversations, both drunk and sober, about life and politics and anger and love. That night, I opened up about how I was really unhappy at law school. This awareness wasn't enough for me to make a change, which is why there are other steps involved, but it was a start.

Instead of accepting the awareness (Step 2), I suppressed it. I pretended I wasn't feeling this way or that it was okay because nobody likes what they do, and I'll make so much money that it won't even matter. The harder I resisted, the harder everything became. It was like quicksand taking me down and the more I struggled to break out of it, the harder it pulled me. So, the harder I drank and partied.

I would go on dates with a guy I was seeing the entire time I was in London and be still awake from three nights of partying, sweating out booze from days prior and not able to hold a conversation. I hit a point where, once I started drinking, I couldn't stop. Except, I couldn't *not* start. As soon as the thought of drinking came into my head, I felt relief. The decision was made. It wasn't a choice anymore. I lost the power to choose. I tried so hard to get through the week without drinking. I just needed to study really hard for a few days and it would be okay. The drinking continued to creep in and the weekends and weekdays became no different from each other. I ended up in the hospital several times because I would party until my body shut down. Then, the first thing I would do when I came out of the hospital would be to pick up a bottle on the way home.

One night in April, I was on a huge bender weekend and made a lot of embarrassing decisions that were hitting all of my shame triggers (my lack of self-worth, my inherent feeling of being no good, of everyone finding out I was a fraud). I was continuing to drink by myself in bed (the main way I drank at this point), and I was starting to black out. I was sort of living in a "brown out," where I wasn't always blacked out, but I was definitely not really present in my life. I was really, really low and couldn't take the pain anymore. I remember consciously thinking it would be best for everyone if I just took the bottle of OxyContin I had from a bike accident a few weeks earlier. I finished another bottle of wine before taking the pills, texting the people I loved to say that they would be better off without me, and hoping to never wake up again.

I woke up in the hospital. I don't remember much. Apparently, I had been coherent for a bit, but I didn't know what had happened. I had freaked everyone out and definitely scared myself. I wasn't surprised it had happened – I had thought about it several times – but I didn't understand the magnitude of the decisions I was making because I didn't feel I was making them. I just knew I didn't want to feel the pain I was feeling anymore. It was too much; I couldn't handle it. My addiction had fully taken over and was going to kill me. The first thing I did when I left the hospital was grab a bottle of vodka on the way home.

The fun party girl was gone, to say the least. I was no longer fun to be around. Friends asked me not to come to parties. My parents ended up coming to London to move me home because they knew I was not functioning anymore (and I think I may have called them drunkenly one night to come get me). I don't remember the phone call but soon enough they were on a flight over, much to my surprise and relief.

I'd be able to pull it together for a few weeks, and then it would fall apart again. The thought would come in and I couldn't stop it. I hated being in my head. I couldn't stand myself or my thoughts and I needed to escape. Except the scariest thing started to happen – I felt the same way when I was drunk as I did when I wasn't. I was just as anxious, just as depressed and the solution to life I had found was not only not working, it was destroying me.

I was back in Toronto and not functioning. One awful day, my grandfather fainted and went to the hospital. I snuck a bottle of whiskey into my purse and continued to pretend to my parents that I didn't know why I seemed drunker and drunker. Then I just sort of let it all out to my dad. I think it was the first time I admitted I thought I might have a problem with alcohol. A few days later, I went to my doctor and he put me on anti-depressants and said that I couldn't drink for the month I was on them. It sounded hard, but I figured I could do it. A month was doable.

My mom decided that we should get away for a bit. I think it was her way of sending me to rehab, but she wasn't capable of letting me out of her sight that month. So, together, we went to the health resort, Canyon Ranch. While we were there I was starting to connect. I was writing in my journal every day, learning how to meditate and exercising for the first time in years. I woke up early, went for hikes and was feeling like I was getting in touch with myself again. I wrote in my journal one day that I hadn't felt this connected to myself in my entire life. It is amazing what a few days of actually putting down the screens and booze and removing yourself from the outside world will do.

On the timetable for the week was a recovery meditation group. It was in the meeting room I had been going to for meditation, so I figured it was a different type of meditating. Little did I know that I was about to set foot in my first 12-step meeting. I was greeted with kindness and open arms, and my mom was with me. We decided to stay and see what it was all about. I felt instantly at ease. Shelly, the woman who shared her story, paralleled me in so many ways. She was older than me and had stayed sober for 13 years. Her story showed me what my life would look like if I continued drinking, but also what it could look like if I stopped. I had a glimmer of hope.

I had coffee with Shelly at Canyon Ranch and told her everything that was going on in my life. She was enormously supportive and understanding, and I felt safe with her. I had never shared some of the things I was sharing with her, and I couldn't pinpoint why. What I know now is she is a deeply authentic and genuine person, and I felt that. I had never heard someone share their experiences with so much courage. I couldn't imagine ever telling anybody the things she told me, and she did it in a way that let me know she had healed. She shared her story with ease and comfort because it had no hold over her anymore. I wanted the grace that she had.

I took the Big Book of Alcoholics Anonymous home with me from that retreat, and Shelly continued to chat with me. My month of no drinking was coming to an end. It was approaching the Canada Day long weekend, and I was having some friends up to my family's cottage. I told Shelly that I was doing well, so I was going to have just one or two beers with my friends on Thursday night. She didn't try and stop me because she knew I needed to experience my journey in my own way.

Those beers were the beginning of the end. I went on a week-long bender. I was an absolute shit-show. I had massive, almost relationship-ruining fights with my sister and mom. I remember my sister begging me to stop, yelling at me and asking why I couldn't see what I was doing to my family. I continued to drink. I locked myself in my room. My mom slept on the couch to make sure I couldn't get to the liquor cabinet, and I would literally crawl on the floor to sneak behind the couch to the kitchen to get more. Like, pardon me? That is absolutely insane. I was way past out of control. Finally, that moment came. The moment when I knew it had to end. As I looked in the mirror, I was reminded of the hope I had experienced at Canyon Ranch, and I wanted it back. I saw the glimmer of my authentic self that was starting to show through the cracks as my ego was breaking. I was splitting into pieces and it was the only way my true self was able to shine out and help me. I have tears streaming down my face as I write this, as that moment changed everything for me.

I accepted the reality of my situation. And this is why acceptance is crucial. I stopped resisting. I was done. Then, I surrendered. I stopped fighting myself and the world and everyone in it. I let go of control and I asked for help.

There was another very synchronistic moment after this surrender. I was sitting on the patio at the cottage after having this realization and I called Shelly. I was bawling, saying that I was an alcoholic and I didn't know what to do. She calmly replied, "Sweetie, I know, and I am here to help." A moment later, a neighbour from down the road was walking her dog past my cottage. Nahanni is this beyond-stunning actress who I had been drawn to for as long as I could remember. Something about her energy was intriguing and mystical to me. I always found myself watching her at parties and wanting to engage in conversation with her but felt weirdly ashamed every time I did. I know now this is because she too radiated the confidence that you only can when you are living in your authentic self. She had been sober for 27 years at this point and was the only honest and "out" sober person that I knew of at the time. I asked her for help. We walked and talked for hours; she told me her story and I told her mine. I once again felt safe with her. I had two women who were carrying me through with love and support and it was exactly what I needed. I just had to be open, honest and willing to hear what they were saying, take their suggestions and do the next right thing.

Everything from this point forward became practice. Sobriety takes practice. Integrating new habits takes practice. I was learning how to live in a completely different way. I had to redefine my life, and in that, I found that I was actually just moving closer to who I really was all along. I wasn't letting go of Dani, I was letting go of an old version of a girl who never really lived in the first place – a girl who merely existed.

I was living in my addiction. I had no way to access the other parts of myself in order to heal, let alone access my authentic self. So, where does that possibly leave someone? It left me starting from the beginning. From being honest, and from surrendering. Soon, I would learn how this girl came to be, and how to get back to who I really was.

The Foundation

An Overview: The Layers of Self

The privilege of a lifetime is to become who you truly are.
– C.G. Jung

Welcome home. This book will take you on a journey of healing the layers that are preventing you from meeting your authentic self and from becoming who you are really are. It will allow you to create tunnels of light through the darkness and align yourself with your authenticity.

I encourage you to read the book from start to finish and do the exercises that resonate with you in each moment. Try them all and incorporate the ones that work for you into your daily routine. This journey is not linear and once you have read the book through, you may need to come back to some areas or spend more time in others. It is your process and there is no right or wrong way. It is important for me to meet you where you are at, right in this moment. Know that you are perfect the way you are, and are transforming, growing and changing in the natural ways that we do in our lives.

Addictions

Defences

False Selves

Core Beliefs

Shame   Shadow

**AUTHENTIC
SELF**

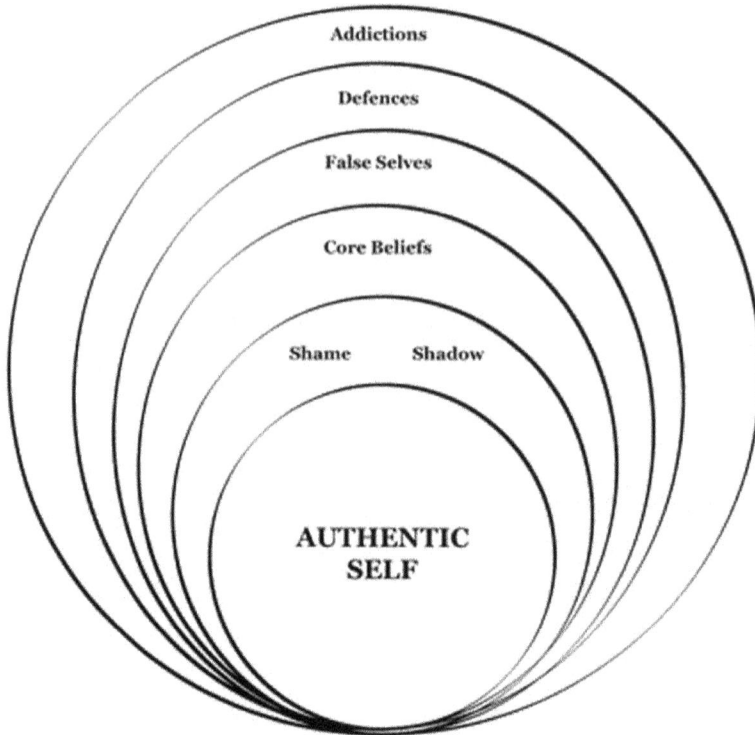

At our core is who we really are – our authentic selves. When we come into this world we are pure love. We soon add a layer of shame and shadow, covering our authentic self. Our core beliefs follow, which begin to create our false selves, what we call our "personality." Defences are built from our personality traits and when they fail to keep us safe, we resort to addiction.

We will start this journey by looking at authenticity, what it is and how to know you are feeling it. There is no point in going through an entire process without knowing what the freedom you will feel on the other side will look like, right? So, the program starts with looking at our authentic selves and essence, and then working our way out. Our most pressing issues are typically the outer layers; however, there needs to be a deeper awareness of how and why those issues have come to be. The layers are created by building upon themselves, so it makes sense to work our way outward! In Chapters 6 to 10, I will explain each layer in detail and give you tips on how to move through them. Your job is to stay open, willing and honest. This is your journey back to you.

- Two -
Our Essence. Our Truth.
Our Authentic Selves.

To be yourself, you have to know who you are.
– Deepak Chopra

Who am I? I used to answer that question like this: I am Danielle McCarron. I am a 23-year-old law student. I like to party. I am a lot of fun. I have a good family and lots of friends. I enjoy skiing, partying (it's really important to me) and travelling.

Then, it shifted to: I am Danielle McCarron. I am 28 years old. I am a mom to Sunny, my Golden Retriever. I am a therapist. I am a health coach. I am a recovery advocate. I am kind and compassionate. I am sober. I enjoy meaningful conversations and exploring the world.

Except, these are external characteristics. Me, who I really am at my core, has never changed. That person is ever-present and never-changing. The external stuff is just that – external stuff. It doesn't mean the material world is not important and I am not belittling our need for the external. However, these are ways of expressing myself. And as I change, they change. Everything external is impermanent, and who I really am is the only constant.

Therefore, I am so much more than these external characteristics. I am more than what I do. I am more than my job. I am more than my past. I am more than what I can actually describe. I am more than what my ego can wrap its little (and sometimes big) head around. I am not my thoughts. I am not my feelings. I am not my body. I am so much more. I am the observer of it all. I am knowing. I am truth. I am love. I am consciousness. I am everything. I am nothing. My authentic self is who I truly am.

My authentic self is all-knowing, ever-present and eternal. It is my spirit. It is my soul. It is a little piece of the universe. If I am living in my authentic self, anything is possible. If everybody in the world lived from authenticity rather than ego, we would know peace. Every job would be filled, every person would be loved. We would naturally flow through life with ease and pure joy. Of course, that is not how life currently is, but by awakening this part of ourselves, we can transform our lives and the lives of those around us.

This is how we come into the world, but something changes along the way. We begin to cover this person up. We cover it up with layers of stuff that isn't really ours. It isn't who we are. The layers are our protection and our experiences. They are our survival instincts exacerbated, they are trauma, shame, guilt and pride. They are what makes up our ego. They are our story.

Our authentic selves then get buried under these layers and conditions. We become disconnected from our truth and live on autopilot. Years of experiences, conditioning, social norms and intergenerational trauma (experiences that have happened to your parents and their parents that have nothing to do with you but have really shaped your life more than you know) have hindered us from living life authentically, from living in our truth.

This journey will bring you to that truth. It will give you the tools to align with who you really are and to tap into that knowing at any point. You will be able to live life out of love, rather than fear, experience a deep love for yourself and the world around you, find your purpose and make the changes you need to make in your life to be the best version of yourself you can possibly be.

We can live life as the person we really are – who we are meant to be. We can know pure joy. We can trust that we will get through the pain. We will know the next right thing for us to do for ourselves, and we will be able to do it with love.

When I am not connected to my authenticity, or "in alignment" with authenticity, life can get pretty rough. I hurt people. I can be extremely selfish. I am fearful. I over-think. I stress right the fuck out. I don't have faith that things will work out or that I can handle what life is throwing at me. I make promises I can't keep. I lack compassion for myself and others and I just can't seem to access my self-love through all of that.

You will learn how to tap back into your authenticity and realign yourself as we move through the ego and blocks. I know this is possible because I am living in that reality. I mean, in no way, shape or form have I mastered anything or don't screw up all the time.

I fall into fear constantly. I am continuously meeting other parts of myself that I was not aware of. I am on this journey, too, and I believe the journey will continue throughout my entire life. However, I now know how to realign myself and make those shifts faster and more consistently. Now, I have the tools to deal with life on life's terms. Now, I can tap into my authentic self when I find myself misaligned with my truth and can put things back into perspective. Now, I can live my best life.

So, what does authentic living look like? I can tell you how it feels for me. Authentic living feels like I am walking through a forest with a compass. Sometimes, the path is clear, the sun is shining and I am confidently walking a comfortable path filled with ease and light. Sometimes, the path splits in several directions and I am really trying to keep the compass at due north. I try and take the right path and keep heading in the right direction. Sometimes, I decide to ignore the compass completely and take a path that is going in the opposite direction of where I am being guided. I take the paths that lead me astray, but eventually, after trudging them, they will circle back to the main road. At times, the path will be completely blocked by trees, I can't seem to find due north at all, everything seems unclear and I can become very afraid. Then, I will notice a glimmer of light ahead, the compass will point to due north and everything will be clear and free again. This is what living an authentic and aligned life feels like.

Authentic living is the cornerstone of being who you really are. Of not being defined by the external – by your job, social status, relationship status or anything else. By removing the layers, you will create a channel that will allow your truth to shine through. You will then have a choice: to choose love over fear. To choose compassion. To choose courage and bravery and vulnerability. To choose you, each and every day. Maintaining this is tough. It will come and go, sometimes a million times a day. But with the tools you will have, you will be able to check back in with *you*. To make decisions that are true for you. It takes practice and daily maintenance to get there. It takes making tough choices. It takes learning to say no to what is no longer serving you and learning to say yes to your truth.

How do you know if you are in alignment with your authentic self? And by alignment, I mean literal alignment. Like a path has been carved between the outside world, through your layers to your authentic self, and from your authentic self to the universe. When we are in complete alignment, miracles happen. We feel it. We know. Miracles are happening. We are open to synchronicities (meaningful coincidences) and possibilities. We are free from attachments, from fear, and we are living in pure love.

How do you live in pure love? You release the blocks. To move through the blocks, follow the four steps outlined in the next chapter, with varied practices, tools and prompts within each.

- *Three* -
The Four Steps of Transformation

Step 1: Awareness (Getting Honest with Yourself)

We cannot change what we are not aware of, and once we are aware,
we cannot help but change.
– Sheryl Sandberg

In my experience, no change can occur without awareness. Awareness is the first step to take for any shifts to occur within us. I had to become aware of my alcohol and drug addiction before I could surrender and admit that I needed help. I was never honest with anybody about this, let alone myself. I figured alcohol was becoming a problem in my life, but it didn't feel like I could be an addict. When I finally hit my bottom, it was clear that alcohol was ruining my life, and it had taken everything from me. I didn't realize that this was just the outer layer of my problems, and there was so much inner work that still needed to be done. I needed to admit to that humbling defeat and get honest with myself, and then with somebody else, that I had a problem.

What self-sabotaging behaviours are you experiencing that are negatively impacting your life? If you have picked up this book, the likelihood is that you already have an idea of what area of your life you would like to transform. Is there an unhealthy relationship holding you back? Are you becoming someone you don't recognize in that relationship? Is an addiction to a substance or to work making your day-to-day tasks unmanageable? Or maybe you need to release some of that toxic judgment you are holding on to like it is the key to happiness. Become aware of some of the blocks you are experiencing. These blocks might not even be totally clear right now, and that's okay! Maybe it is an area that just doesn't keep working out the way you would like it to, but you're not totally sure why. Through this journey, you will be able to gain clarity on whatever it is you would like to shift.

So, get honest with yourself. Write down everything that comes up. Give yourself a few minutes now to write down all of the shit you want to let go of, or that you are afraid to become aware of. You don't need to share it with anyone, just be honest with yourself. It will help to begin the opening-up process that this book will take you through. What is really holding you back from becoming the person you are meant to become? After all, this whole book is about meeting your authentic self.

Remember to become aware of the good, too. Although we have behaviours we would like to change, we also all have great qualities that need to be addressed. When you are writing down what is coming up for you, don't forget to include what is positive as well. We are really damn hard on ourselves, and this journey is about finding balance.

This is the first step towards making a change in every layer we look at in this book, but also in your life. Each layer has slightly different practices you can participate in to bring about awareness and to make things clear. Bringing about this awareness in an effortless way is the aim. Nothing will be revealed until it is ready. The practices suggested are ways of becoming honest and open to what is presenting itself to you. In the next few pages, I have outlined some great practices to get you started.

Practicing Awareness: Mindfulness

Mindfulness has become super hyped in the last few years, and for good reason. It is the start of living in the present. By bringing our awareness to this moment, we can help bring awareness to what habits, behaviours, thoughts, feelings, stories and actions we need to heal.

Depression stems from living in the past and anxiety is a result of living in the future. When we bring our awareness to the present moment, we can alleviate this stress instantaneously and help shift the behaviours, thoughts or feelings that are pulling us away from the present. More often than not, these behaviours, thoughts and emotions will be related to the layers that you are moving through and healing. I encourage you to really delve into this practice and begin incorporating it into your daily routine. This will be an active process and one that will help you throughout this program.

As you walk, eat and travel, be where you are. Otherwise, you will miss most of your life.
– Buddha

What are some of the ways to become mindful and incorporate mindfulness into our daily life?

1. Noticing your breath. Try taking a few deep breaths in and out, right now. Fill your belly and lungs with air and notice how it feels to breathe in and out. Notice any sensations that come up. Feel the air flowing throughout your body, from your fingers to your toes and release any negative thoughts, feelings or tension that you are experiencing.
2. When you are walking, become aware of how the ground feels under your feet. Bring your awareness to where your feet are. Notice five things around you that are real and tangible, like the shape of someone's glasses or the colour of the flowers or

the smell of the rain. Wherever you are, bring your awareness to the room or space you are in.

3. Become mindful of your eating. This is a huge way to help shift our relationship with food, but also to help bring awareness to the present moment. We eat so quickly and usually without even pausing to notice how it tastes or feels because we are watching a show or eating on the go. Notice how each bite tastes. Notice the smells and sensations that occur with each bite. Try to chew your food upwards of 20 times per bite to not only help with digestion but to really make eating a mindful practice.

4. At any point during the day, simply come back to your breath, for three breaths and bring your awareness to where you are in that moment.

5. Use a mindfulness prayer or mantra to ground yourself. I love this Reiki prayer:

Just for today:
I release angry thoughts and feelings.
I release thoughts of worry.
I'm grateful for my many blessings.
I practice expanding my consciousness.
I'm gentle with all beings including myself.

Pause after every line and let it sink in, releasing feelings and choosing the affirmations given.

Get curious:

Start incorporating the mindfulness exercises into your routine immediately. Take some deep breaths, become present and bring your attention to this moment, right now. Then sit with this question for a few minutes: "Who am I?" Get out your journal and ask yourself the following questions:

- When do you feel most authentic?
- When do you feel you are the best version of yourself?
- When do you feel most like YOU?
- Who are you without speaking about your job, your family, your relationships, without focusing on the external?
- What sparks your curiosity? What sparks your joy? When does your heart and soul feel pure joy?
- Now ask yourself again: "Who am I?"

Get curious! If nothing comes up right away, stay open to it. Be gentle with what, if anything, comes up. Take note of these questions and move through your day with curiosity.

Step 2: Acceptance

And acceptance is the answer to all my problems today.
When I am disturbed,
It is because I find some person, place, thing, situation –
Some fact of my life – unacceptable to me,
And I can find no serenity until I accept
That person, place, thing, or situation
As being exactly the way it is supposed to be at this moment.
Nothing, absolutely nothing, happens in God's world by mistake.
Until I could accept my alcoholism, I could not stay sober;
Unless I accept life completely on life's terms,
I cannot be happy.
I need to concentrate not so much
On what needs to be changed in the world
As on what needs to be changed in me and in my attitudes.
– Alcoholics Anonymous basic text, page 417

The second step for change is acceptance. This prayer sums up acceptance for me in my life and is crucial for me to keep at the forefront of every day. You can come back to this prayer whenever you need to. If this doesn't work for you, find an inspirational quote that resonates with you. Use it every morning, evening and throughout the day in order to come into the present moment and accept whatever situation, feeling or seemingly unchangeable dilemma you are in. It gives me back so much power in my life. It allows me to truly understand that I have the ability to change my perspective, regardless of the circumstances, in order to be at peace. It is my responsibility alone to do that. We have to look at what we have the power to change, and what we do not. We always have the power to change our reactions to situations, and this is the golden truth.

It is important to understand that acceptance doesn't mean we like our circumstances! It doesn't mean that I am actually okay or happy about what is happening in my life. It means that I am moving towards surrender. That I am no longer resisting my current situation. It means that I am choosing to accept the present moment for exactly what it is, and that it is exactly as it is meant to be.

Accepting What I Cannot Change

I was in a relationship with a man who was also in recovery from addiction. Peter has been a huge part of my story and journey in recovery. Shortly after we got together, he relapsed. He went back to treatment fairly quickly and things turned around. We moved in together not long after and started building a really beautiful life.

Things were going well. I was back in school studying spiritual psychotherapy at the Transformational Arts College in Toronto, and Peter seemed to be doing well. I was really, really happy. I was having a conversation one day in March 2016 with a woman at school. We were gabbing on about our boyfriends and I was beaming about how lucky I was to have a partner who was doing so well and who really "got me." I had found the man that I wanted to spend my life with. We were both sober and I was envisioning us making plans for our future together.

I took the subway home from school that day and was messaging Peter about what we were going to have for dinner. He was picking me up from the subway and we were going to go to the grocery store, so I was making a list and killing some time on the train.

I sent him a message to let him know I had arrived at our subway station. No answer. I figured he was just driving. A few more minutes went by and I hadn't heard from him. I tried calling, no answer. Weird. Maybe he fell asleep? He passed out hard and fast sometimes.

After 30 minutes of waiting (it might have been less, but it felt like an eternity in my anxiety) I called my mom who lived around the corner and asked her to grab me. Something wasn't right. I was getting really, really scared. My mom asked me if I thought he might have relapsed, but I figured there was no way. Maybe he was in a car accident? I called again, and he answered. My deepest fears came true at that moment. He was high. Everything was spinning. I became nauseated and collapsed. I was not equipped to deal with this.

Flash-forward a year. Peter would have a few months of sobriety here and there and then everything would come crumbling down. Eventually, I moved back in with my parents and Peter and I took some time apart. I went away with some girls to Costa Rica, which was already planned, and took some time for me. So, what happened? My experience of being in love with an addict was much more painful than that of my own addiction. Maybe I just felt that way because it was more recent. Maybe it's because I was sober and could really feel all of the feelings that were there. Or maybe because loving someone else is the most vulnerable act we can experience, and it can nearly take us out if it falls apart, regardless of circumstances.

For the duration of our relationship, I had been trying to control Peter's addiction. I did pretty much every textbook "crazy girl" thing you can imagine. I left. I would threaten to leave and didn't. I yelled, I cried. I looked through his phone. I tracked his phone. I called his family. I called his sponsor. I called him 100 million times a day. If I could only change this one thing then this time it would be different. If I could get him into this treatment centre or that treatment centre, or hook him up to chat with this sober man or help him change his diet or exercise… or… and… or… and… Enough. I was exhausted.

I looked in the mirror and I didn't recognize myself again. I was so sick and tired of being sick and tired. Something had to change. This time, I knew that *something* wasn't my partner. It had to be me.

I reached out for help. I had been here before and was finally willing to take a look at myself. I had been speaking with a couple of women I trusted wholeheartedly during this entire process who carried me through. I admitted defeat and joined a 12-step support group for families of addicts. I began to gain some of my power back. I began to recognize myself again.

I learned about an entire other area of my life that I am powerless over. Ultimately, I realized that I have absolutely no power over anybody else but me. I lost myself completely, even after doing so much work on myself. This made me look harder at myself than I ever had before. It made me dig deeper. It made me trust the universe in a way I didn't know was possible. The result: I began to accept life on life's terms in a profound new way. I made the connection between my head and my heart, and that I am responsible for my own actions and choices. It's not the responsibility of my partner, in any way. He is on his journey, and I am on mine, and by trying to control him and doing every single crazy-girl thing you could possibly think of in order to "save" him, I no longer recognized myself. Three years after I came into sobriety myself, I hit rock bottom again.

I will reiterate that what I did have the ability to control was my reaction to his addiction. Being a healthy example for someone else is the most supportive thing you can do for them. Not by dictating what they need to do, but by demonstrating through attraction and leading by example that this is an easier, much more beautiful way to live.

I was done trying to change him, and if I could not accept the situation I was in, it was my responsibility to change it. That's why this step is so important. It allows us to become clear on what we can accept and live with, and what we have a responsibility to change. I became aware of all of my "crazy" and wrote it down and shared it with someone who had been through the same thing. Someone I trusted. I accepted that this was my reality right now, that I had the ability to change my circumstances and, if I did stay, that it was my choice. And that's the beautiful thing about this step: When I accept life on life's terms, I regain the power of choice. I am no longer a victim of my circumstances. I can connect with my authentic self and my truth — and be free. Acceptance prayer, on repeat. Serenity prayer, on repeat:

God, grant me the serenity to accept the things I cannot change, the courage to change the things I can. And the wisdom to know the difference.

Through acceptance I can always find freedom, I can always find joy, I can always focus on being present and taking care of me. It helps let go of the crazy and bring into focus what really matters.

It reminds me that, through it all, I can thrive, survive and live a really great life.

Step 3: Action – Surrender

Surrender comes when you no longer ask, "Why is this happening to me?"
– Eckhart Tolle

This leads us to the action steps. The action steps will be different for each area of the book and will build upon each other along the way. The awareness and acceptance pieces are crucial to get you to the action piece. They will not be enough without actually doing something to make the changes.

There are three frogs on a lily pad. The first one decides to jump off. How many are left?
Three. The first one only decided to jump.

To surrender is an action in itself; a continuous action and choice we can make to release whatever it is we are holding on to. The word "surrender" has a negative connotation to it in a lot of areas of life – it implies giving up. That is true. To surrender is to give up. However, it is also to give in to each and every moment exactly as it is. To release our hold on how things "should" be and to open up our lives to how they are beautifully unfolding on their own. It is to release our grip, to cease fighting, to let go of the resistance we have to change. When things are changing and we don't like it, we tend to strangle them until there is no life left in them. To surrender simply means to do the opposite of resist. What we resist, persists. The deeper the surrender, the deeper the connection to self. The deeper the surrender, the deeper the peace.

I had to surrender to the idea that I could not control my own addiction. I had to surrender to the fact that I could not control Peter's addiction. I have to surrender to my unhealthy behaviours, my judgment, my fears, my attachment to outcomes, my attachment to my plan for my life, my expectations, my inability to control traffic. I have to surrender constantly.

Surrendering is one of the hardest, but most important, aspects of change. We need to let go of the old behaviours, the old thoughts and the old situations, and admit that we are not able to control what we are trying to control. The axiom is that in letting go, we actually allow natural order to take place. Our authenticity will come through and we will feel more empowered than we knew we could be.

I have to surrender to so many things on a daily basis. When I surrender, I can accept the reality of my circumstances. I can have profound shifts in perception. I can surrender control and surrender my powerlessness. I can ask the universe for help. Sometimes this happens in one deep surrender, but more often than not, it is a daily process. The deeper I surrender, the deeper my connection to myself and my higher power becomes. Then, I am able to delve further into my authenticity and remain aligned more consistently.

Each layer you will move through will have different areas to surrender to. You will be guided through the whole process.

Step 4: Healing

The wound is the place where the light enters you.
– Rumi

All of these steps are null if we are not vigilant about maintaining them. Some things will be removed quite quickly and might not come back. When I moved into a sober life, I surrendered my dishonesty. In that surrender, it never resurfaced. I breathed honesty and never looked back. Other layers take a lot of time and work to move through. My judgment is an example of a component of my character that I have to surrender all of the time; it is a work in progress. Be patient with yourself and use the suggestions that work best for you. I have laid out a ton of maintenance tools that I use, and within each layer there are uniquely tailored maintenance steps to help you live in your authentic truth.

Find a daily practice that works for you. This could be incorporating one of these activities into your routine every day or week. Keep adding more of the good rather than looking at removing the bad. The point of all of this is to add so many good, positive and healthy routines to your day-to-day life that there isn't even room for the unhealthy ones. This process takes away the shame and blame of the unhealthy habits we have learned and helps shift us into a self-love mindset and belief system.

I will discuss this step in Chapter 11 in much more detail. Each chapter will now contain the steps of change in order to release what is blocking us from who we really are. The final chapter will bring everything we have learned together and help you heal and live in that freedom.

Healing takes time, along with awareness, acceptance and action. Trust the journey and have faith.

- *Four* -
Opening to Spirituality

It's always darkest before the dawn.
— Florence Welch

I was cut off from my spirituality for a very long time. I remember feeling at peace in the church as a child, but that was about the extent of my belief in something bigger. Prayer was something I began to actively reject after some bad stuff started to happen in my life, and really, I only prayed for selfish things before that anyways. Once I became aware of the suffering in the world, I denounced my religious affiliations (I was raised Catholic) and thought that if you believed in God, well, you were stupid. There was no way a God could exist with the kind of suffering that was happening to me and in the world.

Spirituality now is the key to authentic living for me. All it means to me is to be open to something greater than myself. Most of the time, that means that I am being open to love — simply choosing love over fear. The spiritual alignment process always comes when I choose love over fear. It comes easily, with watching the ocean waves, the moon and stars in the sky or the beauty of nature. I feel it most powerfully when I am in the presence of all that I, or man, did not create. That's where the magic is for me. I will use the words "the universe" and "higher power" or "love" to describe this knowing throughout the book. Ultimately, it is some form of consciousness that is bigger than me, and that is all that matters. It is something that I cannot wrap my head around, and that is why I rejected it for so long because I was living completely and solely in my thoughts and self. Prayer and meditation are active parts of this program and were crucial in accessing my authentic self. Explore the possibility of using prayer and meditation if you are not used to these practices.

Get curious:

Find what works for you. Get out your journal and write down experiences that you have had in your life where you knew there was something bigger. This might be a walk along the beach, a drive through the mountains. It could be experiencing the deep feeling of love, an unexplained emotion that is so much bigger than us. It could be witnessing the kindness of strangers, or a deep, authentic connection. Whatever a higher power looks like to you it is only important that you are not it, and it is not someone else. You can define it in whatever way you need to and substitute the words I have used in this book for a language that defines this knowing for yourself.

Beginning to Disconnect

I experienced fainting spells throughout my life. They started when I was a child. The first time it happened was in music class in Grade 6. I remember the day clearly – I was wearing overalls and was trying to take them off because I was overheating so bad. My vision went fuzzy, like everything was white and blurry. I blacked out and my music teacher had to carry me to the secretary's office to call my parents.

The next fainting spell was in Grade 12. I was in the kitchen at home when I started to feel a bit dizzy, so I tried to walk upstairs to my room to lie down. When I got to the top of the stairs, I fainted and fell all the way back down the stairs. I hit my head so hard I had a seizure. My sister found me and called an ambulance and the next thing I remember I was coming to with paramedics around me, carrying me out of the house.

The cycle continued. Every few years I would faint, until I was in my third year of my undergraduate degree and I fainted seven times in two months. The episodes were happening more often and the attacks were feeling uncontrollable. The doctors always chalked it up to me being a young girl or being on my period, or partying too much the night before, or having low iron.

It came to the point where I truly believed I wasn't going to wake up again. On top of that, it is a feeling of absolute defeat to know in your heart and soul that there is something wrong with your body but that no one will take you seriously. You think you are crazy. You believe that you are going to have to live this way forever, that it's all in your head. This experience detached and isolated me in so many ways.

The last episode led me to the doctor who finally decided that there was no way this could be chalked up to "just fainting."

A few weeks after being put on a heart monitor, he diagnosed second-degree heart blocks, a condition affecting the electrical system of my heart. Every once in a while, this system would experience a block and the blood would not be pumped efficiently to my brain. The fainting spells were short enough that there wasn't any permanent brain damage at this point, but if they continued, eventually blood wouldn't be pumped to my brain for long enough and I would not recover. I was told that I would need to have a pacemaker implanted into my chest. I was 21 years old and was utterly confused. Wasn't a pacemaker for like, 90-year-olds? Yep. It was. I am consistently the youngest person in the waiting room at the pacemaker clinic, that's for damn sure. The pacemaker was implanted in October 2011 and I haven't fainted since.

Gratitude doesn't begin to describe the space in my heart I hold for the doctors who helped me. I am so blessed that I was "fixed." That said, I was not in a place of gratitude following my surgery. I pretended everything in life was still normal and didn't acknowledge the experience I had just had. I developed severe anxiety and a panic disorder quite soon after. I disconnected from my body. I felt like I was having out-of-body experiences quite regularly. I couldn't get grounded. I didn't even know what being grounded was. I just knew that every time I felt a little bit off, I thought I was going to faint and eventually die. I genuinely believed that I was dying during these panic attacks.

This experience led to an existential crisis. I was living in fear, constantly. I didn't want to talk about it because I understood that vulnerability was a weakness. Feeling fear, pain or vulnerability was not a strength and I couldn't show it to anyone. I needed to suck it up and realize that life happens and I just had to handle it. I didn't think there was anything good about having a pacemaker; I felt that having a physical ailment made me weak. This was not a conscious thought, but in hindsight, I was too afraid to deal with any of it. I started to fear everything. I didn't want to go on the subway for fear of feeling panicky or that I would faint.

I should reiterate that I have not fainted since the surgery and everything I have experienced since was all panic and anxiety related. But, my fear was leading me to have episodes that looked the same. The brain is a powerful tool and can tell us anything – a belief is a thought that we tell ourselves on repeat. Now, my ego was officially running the show.

The Ego

The presence of fear is a sure sign that you are trusting in your own strength.
— A Course in Miracles

Our ego is the part of us that isn't really us. It is the layers, the inauthentic pieces. The ego is trying to keep us protected and safe, but it can also keep our authentic selves deeply buried.

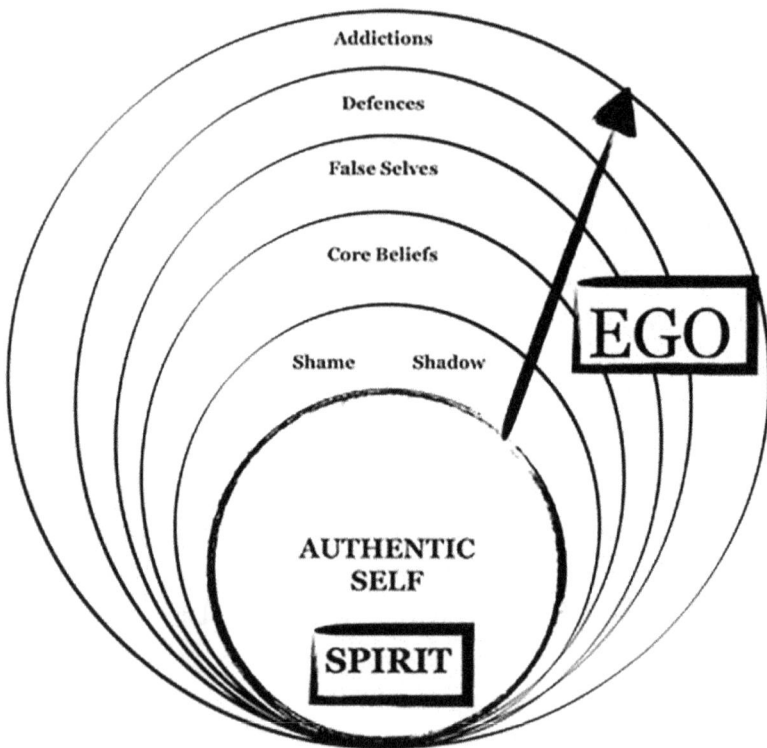

After my surgery, I don't believe I had very many authentic moments. I was cut off. Completely blocked. I did not know how to process the pain I was experiencing or my very real fears. All of the layers, all of the blocks, fears, resentments, judgment and pain.

I didn't have access to healthy, authentic decisions or relationships. I based all of my decisions on external validation.

Externally, I appeared to be okay — thriving even — but I had shut down internally. Eventually, what worked was alcohol. If I kept drinking through the panic, the hangovers, the fear, I didn't have to feel the pain anymore. I wasn't present, I could numb out and pretend that I was "normal" and everything was amazing.

I had coped the best way I knew how. Riddled with anxiety and depression, I felt hopeless. The ego doesn't want to destroy us, it wants to protect us, but our authentic self in alignment with the universe knows how to run our lives better than anything or anyone else. Our ego is a part of us but has a lot of pieces of outside conditioning that are not who we really are.

I was having an existential crisis. I had a breakdown one night because I wasn't even capable of looking at the stars. They seemed so scary. I couldn't wrap my head around the vastness of the universe and what it all meant. It all seemed like too much. I relied solely on intellect, impulsive and irrational decisions and, ultimately, fear. There were real, scary, life-threatening situations happening in my life, and I continued to operate in the only way I knew how – to numb, run and hide. This, of course, caught up with me, and thank God it did. I felt so scared, so alone and it was destroying my life.

The anxiety and depression that stemmed from all of this was due to a lack of connection with my authentic self, and a lack of connection to something greater. It came from a complete disconnect that occurred due to shame, trauma, layers of conditioning and blocks and suppressed emotion. I had disowned parts of myself and my story, and my survival mode was taking over. It came from having zero trust in something bigger working in my life. It came from a lack of authentic connection, a lack of self-worth, an attempt to do everything myself and living in total fear. I was relying on myself, but I couldn't actually handle anything. So where did that leave me?

From this crisis came a beautiful spiritual awakening. Once I began to get honest, remove the layers blocking me from my authentic self and became comfortable sitting in discomfort, my life dramatically changed. I no longer have a complete reliance on myself, but a complete reliance on something else, on my authentic self and the universe. When I align authenticity with the universe, the ego helps me; it doesn't hurt me.

I still struggle with anxiety, but now I use it as a tool. I use anxiety to try and help me figure out what is really going on. It is an indicator that I am being triggered. It is an indicator that I am falling back into relying on self. It is a reminder that I am not fully in the present moment, that I am likely living in the future, in the "what ifs." I still have major worries and pain and operate out of fear. I am human. I can recognize these moments faster and faster and the ebbs and flows are not so dramatic. I can recognize when my ego is running the show by acknowledging my shame and fear and asking myself the right questions to pull out of it before it takes over entirely. If I can't do this, I ask for help. Asking for help is something I need to do on a regular basis and has saved my life, several times.

Being in Alignment

When I am in alignment, things happen effortlessly. All of the career moves or schooling I have done since opening up have happened with such clarity. They have fallen into my lap in such a way that I had to trust that they were meant for me. Going back to school to become a spiritual psychotherapist happened effortlessly. Of course, you still have to work for what you want. But what is meant for you when you are aligned becomes clear.

I then graduated from the Institute for Integrative Nutrition (IIN) and was curious to expand my knowledge of coaching. In opening up to this idea, I received an email a few days later from the International Health Coach University (IHCU), a new university with a Master's program for IIN graduates that is completed online. I applied and was accepted quickly. This opportunity opened me up to the possibility of travelling, one of the easiest ways for me to stay present and feed my soul. I started looking for ways that I could work abroad, travel and study at the same time.

My good friend, Amelia, had just finished a contract position at her job in Toronto. I suggested this idea to her and she said she knew a guy she used to work with who was teaching English in Korea. She would shoot him a message and see how he got his job. He replied on the same day, saying that he was actually leaving his position soon and they were looking for a replacement. The catch was, they needed to fill two spots and a two-bedroom apartment was included in the contract – they wanted friends or a couple. Amelia was shocked and excited, and told him that she didn't want to be pushy but she was actually asking for her and a friend. We were interviewed a few days later and a few weeks after that we were bringing our visa papers to the Korean Embassy in Toronto.

This experience lined up effortlessly because I was in alignment. It felt effortless and simple because I was living from authenticity. When I moved to London, it never felt right. Moving to Korea came from a place of inspiration and joy.

Through listening to that voice, to my "gut," I grew more than I ever would that year. I was able to work at a school and make a difference in children's lives, do my Master's in health coaching and applied nutrition and write this book while also developing my therapy practice and online business, all in one year. I am creating a life that I love. I am designing a life that is best for me, not a life that is supposed to be lived by someone else's standards. That is the cornerstone of authentic living for me – trusting my own process and doing what I know is best for me. This takes practice, as trusting ourselves can be terrifying, especially if we have made pretty unhealthy decisions for a long time. This is all happening because I am giving myself the time I need to do what is best for me right now, with the complete guidance of my authentic self and connecting with the guidance of the universe.

I never, ever regret a decision I make when my authenticity is leading the way. I never, ever will. Because I will always be doing what is best for me. I hope to help you access that authenticity and live in the freedom I have found.

"To thine own self be true."

True that.

Five

Connection, Attachment and Letting Go

True belonging doesn't require that we change who we are; it requires that we be who we are.
— Brené Brown

The Need for Connection

Love and connection are the desire and the drive to bring you closer to another human being for the purpose of being taken care of or taking care of. A baby is completely dependent on its parent for all of its essential survival needs – food, shelter, love, everything. A baby cries through the night because it needs the connection with its parent, or because something is wrong. A baby stops crying through the night when a parent hasn't come for a few nights to hold them. This is not because the baby has learned to cry itself to sleep, it is because they have given up hope. This is a connection break, which adds to our disconnect with self.

As we grow up, our need for connection never goes away. A child will toy with the idea of saying no to their parents in their terrible twos phase, or rebel as a teenager, but the love and need for connection are ever-present. Somewhere along the way, however, we develop some beliefs about this essential need.

A connection is defined by world-renowned shame researcher, Brené Brown, as "the energy that exists between people when they feel seen, heard and valued; when they can give and receive without judgment; and when they derive sustenance and strength from the relationship."

The sad truth is that we go through life believing that in order to have our core need for connection met, we need to let go of our authentic self. We then perpetuate this cycle of external validation to fill a void for attachment that is inauthentic in nature, because it is based on inauthenticity. This attachment, therefore, will not be a fulfilling connection because it is inauthentic. Our need for connection cannot be fulfilled to its best ability.

It is a core need to be loved and wanted for who we are, not what we do. We overcompensate by "doing" because we do not know how to receive the love we need by simply being who we are. This is because there is a major disconnect between the actions we are doing and the person we are at our core. We cannot receive the love we need based on inauthentic actions; only the authentic action will fulfil our authentic connection needs.

The problem is, this becomes compromised as children in trying to balance our authenticity and connection needs. When our connection to others seems compromised, our self-esteem takes a hit. We store it in our shame, and our shame grows. We then will adapt our behaviour so our connection need will be met in an inauthentic way. From this point on, we will continue to settle for the behaviour of others that consistently attacks our self-esteem, as we feel this is meeting our connection need. Except it isn't. Because it is an inauthentic connection. So, the shame continues to build, our self-esteem becomes more and more buried, and our authenticity cannot shine through.

If we go through life acting from our authentic selves, we will inherently make authentic connections that fill our true connection need. The world needs our authenticity and we are here to reclaim that part of ourselves that we have spent our lives burying.

We believe that we are not worthy of love and connection. We believe we need that love and connection but will not be able to receive it by being our authentic selves.

The Authenticity vs Connection Dilemma

When I was teaching English in Korea, most of my students were three to five years old. I started to notice that each child had their own unique way of getting their connection and authenticity needs to be met. Their internal struggle while trying to achieve these goals was an incredible experience to witness. That said, deciding how to handle it or attempt to handle it by not causing more pain for them was also immensely challenging.

We had this class once a week where we would watch an animated book on a Scholastic website. During this time, the kids would all take turns trying to sit on my lap. I loved cuddling with them and would have loved for all of them to be able to take turns sitting with me, but the reality was that once one did, I would have eight kids crawling on me and not paying attention; it was completely unmanageable.

The interesting part of it was not that they just needed the connection and love from an adult, but the way in which they went about getting this need met.

Elizabeth would always pretend that whatever we were watching was scary so that she could sit on my lap and cuddle up. Kyle would say he had a stomach ache and that I needed to rub his belly for him. Bridget would straight up hit another kid in the class so that I would pull her aside, and then she could hug me to get more attention from me. Nancy was really just sneaky. I never understood how she did it, but she would ask a few questions and then somehow end up lying on my lap before I was even aware it was happening. She was the master at playing this game.

Another method of theirs was, of course, acting out, or repeating behaviour that got them attention. Kyle was the class clown and if I laughed at something, he would do it 200 times over to get the same reaction. The initial act might have been authentic but after that, it became a need for approval and connection.

The school used a star system, where each morning you would draw four stars on the board for each child and then take them away if they misbehave or add more as a reward. So, every morning I would ask them which colour stars they would like. At first, there were always a few kids who picked the same colour. Carly would pick pink every day, or three of the boys would pick the same colour as each other. As time went on, most of them began to follow one child and pick the same colour as him. Elizabeth would, without fail, pick a different colour. Even if all of the other students picked purple – her favourite colour – she wouldn't do it. She wanted to be different. Unfortunately, this beautiful rebellion of authenticity faded as well. The moulding process took place.

These instances happen for every child, and they all develop their own unique skill-set in order to get their needs met at a young age. These children are simply trying to get their need for connection and fulfilment met while maintaining their authenticity. It is an internal battle that sets the tone for the rest of our lives. It is the first disconnect from our authentic selves that occurs and the first component of shame, and I believe it is at the core of so many of our issues as adults today.

So, this poses the question: How can I get my connection needs met while still being my authentic self?

A child's needs are needs of attachment. This is because they are reliant on someone else to fulfil their basic needs. This then develops into a struggle to find their own footing and their own unique selves, while still fulfilling their need for attachment. We are not fully self-sufficient overnight; this doesn't happen until much later in life.

As time goes on, this attachment becomes a need for connection. As the shift occurs, when we aren't receiving authentic connection due to a disconnect occurring, this attachment can become unhealthy, as the need for connection is coming from an inauthentic place. We are no longer reliant on someone else to fulfil our basic needs, but we still put that pressure on other people because of the disconnect that is created.

There is a dramatic difference between attachment and connection as adults that we don't seem to be able to distinguish between:

- The need for attachment comes from a place of fear. The need for connection comes from a place of love.
- Connection is a core need each and every person has. Attachment is the fear of this need not being met.

Believing that my partner is "mine" is an attachment. Fearing he will leave me and becoming possessive or jealous is an attachment. Sharing something vulnerable with him and him responding in a kind and open way is a connection. Needing external validation is an attachment. Having an intimate moment with a friend is a connection.

Get curious:

1. Awareness

You can feel the difference between attachment and connection in your gut. It will feel positive or negative within your physical and emotional self. The exciting butterflies could be connection, where the sinking pit in our stomach is attachment. Think about an intimate moment you have had with someone: a partner, a friend, a stranger. It could be a conversation, a glance, a touch. Connect with the sensory feelings that were induced by this interaction. Find a moment that brought you into the present, that made you feel whole, worthy and enough. That is when a connection is occurring, and our connection need is being fulfilled.

Think of a moment when you felt possessive or controlling over someone or something. When you acted on that feeling, was it out of love, or out of fear?

2. Acceptance

There is always a choice: love or fear. Remember that connection comes from love, attachment comes from fear.

The beautiful gift on the other side is, when you release and surrender the attachment, authentic connection can occur. We can flow and let go of what is no longer serving us.

Some emotional clues that you are holding on to an attachment are:

- Jealousy
- Resentment
- Not feeling good enough
- Feeling rejected

3. Action

So, when did you feel these emotions? They feel pretty yucky, right? Usually gross emotions can be easily traced, but we need to be honest about them! What happened? Write down the story you are carrying about this experience or experiences.

Now, get curious about what the undercurrent of these attachments might be. If you aren't aware of it right now, ask yourself, what if you were aware? Could it be a fear of not being loved? Could it be a fear of abandonment? Get curious about the undercurrent of these emotions and reactions. More awareness will come out throughout this book and opening yourself up to being WILLING to be aware, could be enough to bring this awareness when it is ready.

4. Healing

Where can you own that this feeling wasn't your true self coming through, but a part of you that could use some healing? Send light and love to that part of you. Feel it in your body and envision light going to that place.

Next time these emotions are triggered, pause. Let yourself feel what is going on before you react and ask yourself where this reaction is coming from. Is it from a place of fear or a place of love? When you move through it, you will be able to have deeper, more authentic connections.

Letting Go of Attachment

Being in love with an addict was raw, vulnerable, fearful, crazy-making and addictive itself. When I was in my own active addiction, I was escaping. Although the pain was constantly present and only worsening near the end, I had a numbing and loving companion in alcohol for a long time. When someone you love is in active addiction, there is no escape from that pain. There is no checking out.

My awareness and acceptance of my own addiction came fast and furious. I had that "sky is opening" moment where I surrendered and everything became so clear. That was not the case in my relationship. Little by little, I have deepened my knowing that I am powerless over another's addiction. I could tell you that about any sponsee, client, friend or fellow in recovery. I have had a major blind spot when it comes to my relationship with an addict. It mirrored my addiction to alcohol in far too many ways and brought me back to my knees.

I have always been a caretaker, the ear for someone else's problems, the friend you would call in the middle of the night in a crisis. I still am. However, this can cross into very co-dependent and unhealthy behaviour for me, as I feel the need to run to someone else's rescue. This embodies the caretaker's sub-personality, but we will get into that a bit later. Boundaries are tough for me, particularly when I take on others' pain or problems. It has always been hard for me to know where I stop and another person begins. This stems from the co-dependent relationship I have with my mother. We have always been insanely close, but boundaries have not been a strong point for us. For as long as I can remember, I have taken on my mother's emotions, particularly while she is taking on the emotions and caretaking role for my father. In the relationship that has been mirrored to me, caretaking is how you show your love for someone else. This is not always a bad thing. However, I have taken it to an extreme.

When Peter relapsed the first time in our relationship, I felt deeply that he needed support from me. It was a co-dependent act and one made out of not being healthy enough yet myself to make a different decision. I believed that love was stronger than addiction. I knew deep down that it wasn't enough to see the pain my addiction caused my family to really become accepting of my own addiction and move into sobriety. But, I believed it would be enough for somebody else. I was holding on so tight to the idea of what our life could be that I was missing what was actually happening in front of me. I lost the ability to connect to the truth, or I was unwilling to do so. I was not in the present moment. I was escaping again.

Holding on to something when every sign is telling me to let go is one of the most painful experiences I have ever had.

Awareness is the first step to change. I will keep reiterating that. It is very hard to change what has not come into our consciousness yet. However, when that awareness does make itself known, we have to be willing to listen to it. It is the feeling of having an intuitive moment when you are clear on what the next right thing to do is. You know what your responsibility is. You know what your part is in the entire situation. You must do better when you know better.

The thing is, I didn't. I was too afraid.

The first time I had the intuition to let go of this relationship was about a year ago. Things were going really well, actually, and Peter had been sober again for a few months. I woke up with this awful feeling in my stomach in the middle of the night. I was lying on my side, in bed next to this man whom I loved and was living with, and my instincts were screaming at me that this wasn't right. They weren't saying that he wasn't right for me, or that things might not work out eventually. They were specifically telling me that right now, this relationship wasn't going to work. I went back to sleep and tried to pretend it was a bad dream. He relapsed two weeks later.

Recently, I had the same feeling. He relapsed again, and this time, it made no sense to me. There was nothing I could point to or blame as the "reason" it was happening. I was living abroad, we had just had an amazing vacation together and things were going so well. This time, I couldn't pretend I didn't know better. I knew the moment he picked up his drug of choice again that I could not be in this relationship anymore. That I couldn't go through the turmoil again. That not only did I need to let go of the relationship for myself, but I needed to make the healthier choice for both of us.

The thing is, I didn't.

I loved him and tried to convince myself that I was being compassionate and supportive. In knowing what I know now, one of the ways my ego and rationalizer come into the picture again is by using what I know against myself. I know compassion is a key ingredient in healing addiction, so I tell myself that I am just being compassionate and supportive in order to get what I want, in order to control the situation. That I could maybe live with this and things would be okay. That I didn't need trust in my relationship and I could manage everything. Thank God this insanity only lasted for a month this time. I knew better now, and I couldn't live with the pain of unknowing what I knew. Now that I had this awareness, I had to do something about it.

That's the trickiest part, though – taking action. That is why there is a step in the middle. I had to accept that this was my current situation. I had to accept that for some reason, the universe had a different plan for me. I had to accept that no matter what I did, said or intended, his disease was not in my ability to control or change.

I hit my breaking point and I was able to release the relationship as it was. Will I always have hope for him? Yes. What I have absolute faith in is the way the universe works and brings me just what I need, when I need it. It is my responsibility to maintain my alignment with the universe and act on what it is telling me. The signs became so clear that the action almost didn't feel like it was an action to be made. It was a tiny step in the right direction that made a huge impact on my life. It was a release that felt like it had already been happening for some time. I don't regret a moment, because I was not capable of doing anything any earlier than I did.

Now, what did the signs look like? I am going to attempt to be as clear as I can with the way I interpreted the universe's signs to me.

First of all, every single post on social media was about releasing, letting go, trusting, etc.

The second sign was breathtaking. I was in the Philippines for a long weekend amidst all of this. It was such a gift to be travelling on my own among this chaos. I had time to sit in nature and work through what I needed to work through. One of the suggestions made to me was to write a note to my higher power, turning over or surrendering my relationship to the universe. I did just that. I was no longer going to do what I thought was best, and I was going to listen to what the universe knew was best instead. I had a good cry, signed the letter and burned it on the beach. I released it into the air, over the ocean and went for a walk down the beach. It was a beautiful beach on the north shore of El Nido, Palawan, and there was not a soul in sight. I walked for about an hour and was starting to make my way back. The day felt like it was coming to an end. As I was walking, a cloud passed overhead. I said the serenity prayer out loud. As I released the last word, continuing to walk forward, the cloud seemed to break. It was as if every step I took forward was out of the cloud and into the sunlight. Eventually, I was just ahead of the cloud, walking in the sun, with the cloud streaming behind me. As I continued, it disappeared.

I felt safe. I felt supported. I knew in the depths of my soul that the universe was protecting me, and everything was going to be okay.

Thirdly, and most importantly, my gut was screaming at me to take action. I couldn't deny what my body, intuition and authentic self were telling me any longer. Once I finally took the action I needed to take, I felt a sense of relief. I felt as if I had really let go, transformation happened. I could feel the growth and alignment happening within me.

I know that things are going to work out the way they are supposed to, and if we are meant to be together, we will be.

The thing is, even amongst all of this, the life I have today is more beautiful than anything I could have planned for myself. I never thought I could be fulfilled in the ways that I am. I never thought I would have the ability to really create whatever life authentically worked for me. That life wouldn't be possible if I didn't surrender to the Universe and trust my authentic self.

I am continuously reminding myself that:

- It's okay to be afraid.

- It's okay to be uncertain.

- Letting go leads to freedom.

- Faith is always the answer.

- There is always a choice.

- In letting go of control, I actually gain the control I was trying to get in an unhealthy and inauthentic way.

When I was able to release the relationship, I actually gained everything I was trying to gain while I was holding on to it. I gained freedom. I gained a sense of security. I gained the openness for authentic connection.

By living in faith, and trusting my authentic self and the universe, I have the knowledge and trust now that everything will work out for the greatest good. So many things in my life have not worked out the way I wanted them to, but they have all worked out far better for me in the long run than if I continued down a path that was not meant for me.

By letting go, we make way for the good. We make way for real, authentic connections. We make room for freedom. I was unhealthily attached to my relationship. I wanted it to work out the way I thought was best. I knew I needed to let go, but I was really hoping the universe would let me hold on to this one thing I really wanted. Sorry friends, it doesn't work that way. Attachments have the real ability to destroy us because they trick us into believing the intangible is tangible. Real, authentic connections are the path to freedom. By being healthily detached *and* connected, we can really be true to who we are and live our best, authentic lives.

Get curious:

1. Awareness

In order to take the step forward I needed to take, I really had to look at what was holding me back. It usually comes down to fear. There were some major fears that were hindering me from taking action.

What came up for me when bringing awareness to it all?

The fear of failure. I had spent three years trying to make this relationship work. Now, what will be left of me? I had failed.

The fear of judgment. What will other people think?

The fear of being unlovable. Will anyone else ever want me? Maybe this was the only person who could love me because we have a lot of the same stuff to deal with. Maybe nobody will love me.

The fear I won't get what I want. What if this was my one chance at having a family? What if this means I am going to be in my 30s before I get married? What if I never get married?

Sigh. Release.

If I acknowledge the fears, they don't have the same power over me. When I am honest about them with someone I trust, I can hear the insanity in them. I can hear that they are based on old conditioning. I can hear that they are not authentic needs. I can trust that my authentic needs will always be met when I am in alignment. I can move through them. I can trust that it is okay to be afraid. As American Buddhist Pema Chödrön said, "Fear is moving closer to the truth." That felt very right for me at this point.

What else?

The "shoulds." The "shoulds" came up a lot for me. I *should* be settling down. I *should* be getting married. I *should* be where I am not. (Acceptance prayer on repeat.)

The fear of the unknown. This one is big. I am letting go of something I thought was certain. I like certainty. I am a control freak, after all. I am constantly being pulled by my wanderlust and inner child in one direction, and my controlling, fearful adult who wants everything to be known in the other. When I open myself up to the unknown, it feels exciting now. It doesn't have the same power over me. When I am desperately holding on to something that is no longer good for me, my shame and fears tell me that the unknown is too scary, and it is better to be in known suffering than unknown happiness. I know the suffering, I am familiar with the suffering. Suffering is a core addiction of mine. It all comes back to control.

When I release what is no longer serving me, the unknown becomes beautiful and exciting. A year ago, I could not have told you where my life would be. Three years before, my life looked completely different. With each step forward, in alignment, I now know I am being taken care of and that the unknown is a spiritual truth.

2. Acceptance

Accepting this comes and goes. It is a continuous process. What I have accepted is the present moment for how it is. The known, secure and safe future that I want to hold on to is actually not even real. The picture I painted for myself of our wedding, family and life were not fact. They were fantasy. This doesn't mean that the ability to manifest true desires in life does not exist, it means that the "certain" can become uncertain overnight, and that brings me right back to what I know is the truth. Right here, right now. The present moment. Everything else is unknown. All I can do is what is best for me now and put one foot in front of the other, with faith.

3. Action

Taking the steps to release the relationship was not a swift and easy process. I did the work to help me get there but letting go took a while. It was so painful sitting in that awareness. Finally, the moment came when enough was enough and it had to happen. I felt release.

Letting go can be done in so many different ways. For me, it came with ritualizing the process by writing a letter to the universe. It came with setting boundaries that felt impossible to set. It came by taking each minute, each moment, one at a time. It came by staying present, by staying connected, by trusting.

• Write your own letter to the universe: What do you want to let go of? How do you want to feel?

• Write the letter as if you are already where you want to be. Burn it or put it in a "Surrender-box" – a safe space where you can store anything you need the universe to take care of. You can write down your hopes and dreams, desires you want to manifest (see Chapter 12) or any stressors that you just can't handle on your own and need to get out of your head and surrendered to the universe. Spend some time finding a box that speaks to you.

- Set intentions and goals for what is to come. Redirect the focus to you. It is the only thing we can control, so let's radically focus on us!

- Create a mantra using the present moment. "I am free," "I am sober," "I am happy and independent." See Chapter 11 for more information on using mantras.

- Meditate. Pray. Gratitude lists. Self-care. Repeat.

4. Healing

In letting go, I have to be so gentle with myself. When you are letting go of habits, relationships, jobs or anything that no longer serves you, be gentle with yourself. Self-care is crucial. Take a bath. Go on a trip. Eat ice cream. Go for a run. Do whatever authentically serves you in taking care of yourself through this time. I have had to really take a lot of solo-time lately. I find myself being very susceptible to other people's energies when I am vulnerable, and I really need to nurture myself even more than I usually do.

Self-care is how we take our power back. It is how we put ourselves first. We cannot give to others what we do not have ourselves. We will talk more about self-care in the last chapter of the book.

Each day gets easier. Each day I feel stronger. Each day I feel more connected to my truth. By holding on, I wasn't aligned. I was choosing to be misaligned out of fear. That's okay. I am human. I will hopefully learn from this and be able to move through future situations with a little bit more ease and grace.

Practice: Meditation

This is crucial for healing and maintaining what I have learned. If I am not meditating, I notice my restlessness and discontent. I am not living as authentically as I can and the channel to my authentic self is much more easily maintained when I am actively meditating. I have fallen off at times, and the hamster wheel of thoughts is much harder to slow down when I am not vigilant.

To me, meditation is simply aligning my authentic self with my higher power, the universe, and listening to my truth. It is a quiet time to stop the hamster wheel from spinning in my head, or as my dear friend says, "to quiet the committee living in my brain." It creates space between our thoughts and accesses who we are. Then, it allows us to live in that space. That space is where the magic happens. Meditation is a reprieve for me now from the thoughts. It is not used as an escape, but rather to observe myself and be a witness to the movie of my life.

Meditating does not have to be sitting in silence for two hours every day. It can be that, if it authentically works for you. If you haven't meditated before, I encourage you to listen to some of the meditations on my website. There are basic meditations and you can start practicing them daily for just a few minutes at first. I have an online "learn how to meditate" basics workshop on my website, and in-person/live online workshops available as well. If you have an active meditation practice already, I encourage you to delve deeper into that practice on this journey. Check out daniellemccarron.com for online meditations and guidance in getting started with your own meditation practice. Throughout the book, there are guided meditations to help heal specific areas. They are also all available on my website. I encourage you to give them a try, even if meditation hasn't been your thing before. How will you know if you never try?

The Layers of Self

The First Layer:
Shame and Shadow

*Darkness cannot drive out darkness: only light can do that. Hate
cannot drive out hate: only love can do that.*
— Martin Luther King Jr.

I grew up in an amazing home, with a great family, loving and
supportive parents, and siblings who were my best friends. There
is not one thing I can point to from my childhood that would lead
me to become an addict, besides maybe genetics, as there is a
history of alcoholism on my maternal grandfather's side. This led
to one major question that kept popping up for me in early
sobriety:

Why me?

I have since released this question and accepted my life on its
terms, but it left me curious and intrigued about how a girl with
my background ended up where I ended up. There had to be a lot
of pain there, but it didn't add up.

For me, and so many others, there actually wasn't one huge trauma that took place that led to my addiction. Gabor Maté, the world-renowned addiction specialist, speaks about trauma being the "break" that leads to addiction. I will refer to this break as a disconnect. This disconnect creates the layer of shame we feel and leads to further unhealthy behaviours, defences and so much more built upon the initial disconnect. Addiction is the way we handle our pain. Therefore, there still is pain underlying the addiction.

Take your left hand and hold it in a fist and put your index and middle finger from your right hand on the top of your left hand. Start tapping your left hand with these two fingers. Not overly hard, just start tapping. Keep going. After a while, it starts to tingle and becomes a bit uncomfortable. You can stop at any point, now. But, if you were to keep going, eventually this would leave a bruise. If you went on for years doing this, it might even break something in your hand.

This is what can happen to children who experience trauma. It doesn't have to be one major traumatic moment that we typically envision, it can be tiny taps over time that lead to a disconnect. However, some children can experience a horrific disconnect from their authentic selves that completely blocks the light of their essence from coming through.

Trauma can be experienced in as many different ways as there are people, with different interpretations and experiences. Dr. Maté describes this as children experiencing trauma through something happening that isn't supposed to happen or something that is supposed to happen that didn't. The nature of this idea is that each child will have a different perspective on it, based on who they are at their core, and on other experiences they have had. Some are more sensitive, and some have different needs. We are all unique; the tiny taps might be nothing to one child and cause a complete disconnect for another.

Trauma, therefore, is a series of stressful events or one overly stressful event that we no longer have the capability to appropriately manage. Essentially, our ability to cope is overwhelmed. Trauma will then disconnect us from our authentic selves. It adds to the authenticity vs connection dilemma and creates the layer of shame.

Imagine tiny specks of dirt covering a beam of light. Only one speck at a time needs to be placed over our light, but in time, those tiny pieces of dirt will cover up our authentic selves completely and will create a thick layer of dirt – mud, even. This mud is a thick layer of shame. This shame tells us that we are no good, that our true self is not worthy and that it, not our true selves, will take care of us. It is the first remnants of ego coming out in our lives. It is the first layer that begins to cover up our essence.

Let's say a two-year-old is singing at the top of their voice in a public place. It is extremely challenging for a parent to draw the line between allowing their child the freedom to express themselves and shaming them into not wanting to sing anymore. They might explain to their child that they need to save their singing for when they're at home. This, then, might add a bit of dirt to their light, or a lot of dirt to their shame layer, covering their authentic self. This will continue to happen and will create thin layers of shame. This can happen through parents, grandparents, siblings, other adults, anyone close to the child. The anger that a parent or guardian might exude in explaining this to a child might be more aggressive than necessary. We are trying to mould children to fit into the box society has created for each of us, and in that moulding process, the shame layer builds and a disconnect from authenticity occurs. No matter how amazing a parent you are, it happens. It is part of being human.

To shame their child might not be the intention of the parent. It usually isn't. Regardless of intention, however, this is how it is received by the child. It is an intuitive process of survival for the child and they will unconsciously determine that their need for attachment will not be met if they continue with that behaviour.

So, they suppress it. They disconnect from it, and it is then stored in their shame and shadow. That survival mode continues to take over, even well after the need for it is gone.

This pain is not available to our conscious awareness (meaning, we go through life unaware of this pain). It comes in and affects the present and tears shit up. It infiltrates our lives by building upon itself. It is how we protect ourselves. It is unconscious, but eventually it needs to become conscious in order to heal.

It's true that the pain we experienced as children might have come from our parents. This is due to them passing their awareness of their own pain down to us completely unconsciously. When others act out of their pain, we take that on. It becomes ours. It creates the cycle of inauthenticity and passes pain from parents down to their children. This is how healing our own pain and trauma can ensure that we do not pass it down to the next generation. By being our authentic selves, we can help heal our children, future or present. We don't have to act out of our own pain and hurt others. We can change ourselves to change others.

So then, what is shame? We have discussed how it develops, but we haven't discussed how it manifests or how it feels.

Shame

Shame is the most powerful, master emotion. It is the fear
we are not good enough.
— Brené Brown

I always felt like I was born without a layer of padding. Like things just affected and infiltrated me so much deeper than they did other people. I remember these feelings from childhood. This feeling that there was something deeply wrong with me, and others were going to find out. Where this came from, I have no clue, and quite frankly it is irrelevant. I've accepted it. The point is, I am aware of this feeling now. This was part of my shame layer and as we now know, it could have been built from a million different experiences.

Shame is a feeling deep within us that tells us that we are unworthy. It tells us we are intrinsically wrong, or bad, or will never be good enough. It tells us that we need to hide who we really are, because who we really are is wrong. Guilt tells me that what I did was wrong, and this is the difference between shame and guilt, as shame tells me I *am* wrong. I *am* bad, not what I *did* is bad. It is a core emotion and a direct reflection of myself, not a reflection of an action. Shame is then furthered by a feeling that bad things are happening to me because there is something wrong with me. Shame is one of the biggest barriers to authentic living, as it is in our deepest selves, closest to our essence, and can be a thick, dense layer of shadow, hurt and pain.

How do we deal with this? We create other layers. We further disconnect. Defences. False selves. Sub-personalities. They all start to pile up and develop. Healthy personalities can develop if our authentic self is present and leading the way, but unhealthy patterns and behaviours develop from ego, fear and shame.

I carried so much shame around as a child, and this continued into my youth and adult life. My friendships became inauthentic and were mostly based on a mutual love of partying, and I was judgmental of anyone who didn't fit into that mould. I was running my life out of fear. Fear that you would see who I really am, and I really believed that person was unworthy of your love.

I then made decisions for myself that went against who I really was. I made decisions based on what I thought I should be doing, or what would make me feel better about myself in that moment. It was all about removing pain in the moment, taking me out of the moment, going somewhere else. Escaping. And this is all due to the thick layer of shame I was unconsciously holding on to.

How does shame show up for me today? It is all visible in my negative self-talk. For instance, I missed a phone call with a friend the other day. We were supposed to catch up, it had been a while, and I totally blew it. I was trying to juggle too much, didn't put it on my calendar, and missed our window. If I was feeling guilty about this, my self-talk after would be, "I am trying to do too much right now, I need to apologize and ensure we reschedule." My shaming self-talk showed up, however, and sounded like this: "I am such a loser, I screw everything up. How come I can't do anything right?" Whoa. Super unhealthy and negative chatter happening. This is shame, not guilt.

Some more of my shame dialogue sounds like this:

I left my phone at home, which happens when I am not present and scrambling around. I noticed when I was already at the bus stop and I had to run back and get it. I was already running late. My shame tells me I am so stupid, and why can't I do anything right?

My dad corrected a spelling mistake on my website for me and my next thought was, "I am a failure."

I became very emotional one day at work. So frustrated with a situation, I started to cry. My shame tells me, "Suck it up, don't let anyone see you cry." I was fighting the flu, and my emotions were running high. Shame tells me, "I am weak for getting sick."

Do any of these sound familiar?

I can now recognize when shame is popping up and get curious about what is underlying the issue, because it is never really about the issue in front of me. Like every piece of our ego, it is important to get curious about where this messaging is coming from, and what it's really about.

The best part about shame? It has a kryptonite – there is one thing that shame cannot survive. There is a trick to releasing shame. It is simple and effective, yet probably one of the most challenging things we can do.
So, what is the destroyer of shame?

Honesty.

Shame cannot survive in an honest environment. If we become aware of our shame and are honest about it with ourselves (and for me, that includes being honest with someone else as well) it has absolutely no power over us anymore. Shame needs to hide in the darkness. It hides in the nooks and crannies of ourselves and sucks the light out of us. Honesty creates cracks in the walls. It brings light into the darkness. And shame cannot survive in the light. It is like those weird, horror/zombie movies where the hero finally gets all the monsters into a room for long enough for the sun to come up, opens the curtains, says their cheesy line, and blasts the demons away.

This is what honesty does.

Shame tells me that I am wrong, that I am intrinsically and utterly wrong, and that if anybody sees that part of me, they won't love me. That I am not worthy of love. That I am never going to be enough.
     Then, I continuously act out of shame, to prove that I am enough, or to get my needs met in the unhealthy ways that I know how, and I feel more shame about what I am doing. If I speak to these actions, feelings or thoughts, it doesn't mean that they will never pop up again, but it is the quickest fix for shame, and over

time, those cracks become broken-down walls that vigilant honesty and connection will keep down.

When I was heavily in my addiction, I was incapable of being honest. I could not be honest with myself, let alone anybody else. This enabled my shame and addiction to continue running my life. I would lie because if you saw the real me, you would hate what was inside. Little did I know that my shame was not my authentic self, but it had been running the show for so long I didn't know there was another part of me that I could connect to. I thought that this was me.

The day that I reached out for help and admitted I had a problem with alcohol. That I had been drinking daily for months. That I had been skipping class to drink in bed. That I was getting attention from whoever would give it to me and continuously destroying my self-worth. The moment I admitted this to myself and to someone else, it disappeared. It literally had no hold over me anymore, because I had created a crack. I had broken through the layers and cut right through the shame, and the light of my authentic self was able to come through. I was able to become aware that my behaviour of late was due to trying to get needs met out of fear. I could then accept my past, and I could release it and move forward. That was the glimmer of hope for me, that I could maybe, just maybe, fight this thing. That maybe, just maybe, I was worthy enough to give myself a chance. That I was not destined for the sad, miserable life that I felt I deserved.

Honesty. It is the magic elixir.

Healing Our Shame

Healing shame is a journey, like every other healing process, and it is important to be gentle with yourself through this healing. This is tough, consistent work. It doesn't happen overnight. It requires rigorous action. But, when we become aware of how our shame shows up for us, we can recognize when we are in our shame faster and heal it faster. It is a crucial component of healing and living in authenticity.

Get curious:

1. Awareness
How is shame showing up for you, right now? How are you operating out of a place of shame, rather than authenticity? What does your shame dialogue sound like? Who does it sound like? Does it sound like you? Does it sound like a parent? A boss? A sibling? Has there been an instance lately when you were able to recognize shame-based self-talk? Get curious. Next time you make a mistake, or something isn't going super smooth, notice what comes up. Notice where in your body it feels like it's coming from. Sit with it and honour it. Become willing to see what is underneath.

2. Acceptance
Get honest about it. Share it with yourself, write it in your journal, and then share it with someone you trust. If you don't have someone in your life who will honour where you are at, and not enhance the shame, then that is okay. I will honour your story for you.

3. Action
When shame comes back out, as it will continuously attempt to do, a great tool is to actually speak to your shame, the way you would speak to a person.

"What are you trying to tell me? Oh, that I'm a loser and I don't deserve love? Well, I actually know that I am worthy of love and light and you are not going to have that power over me today. I am setting a boundary and I am not going to take your abuse."

Repeat.

Repeat that you are worthy of love and you are enough. Repeat it over and over until you believe it. Until the shame subsides. Sometimes it will be quick, sometimes it will take more time. But with persistence, it will happen.

4. Healing
Finally, notice how your shame comes out in interactions with others, and how you might be shaming others. What part of you needs to voice this shaming message? What part has been triggered? Get curious, get honest, love yourself through it and release it.

We can use our shame, like every other part of us, as a tool to learn more about ourselves. To learn more about how we have become the people we are today. It is trying to protect us from being hurt, from being vulnerable, from experiencing pain. We can retrain our conditioning, come into alignment with our authenticity, honour it, learn from it and release it.

A tool for healing shame: The mind-body-soul connection
I had severe upper stomach pain for years. It manifested in myriad ways, but mostly, it was severe pain that led to nausea or diarrhoea. I tried everything. It continued well into my sobriety and didn't seem to go away.

The pain occurred in my solar plexus, the part of your upper stomach where you experience anxious butterflies or a "knot." Our solar plexus holds our self-worth and our self-esteem and with that, our fears around our needs and our worthiness. What I recognize this pain as now was severely suppressed emotion.

The pain will come up still when I am not being true to myself. When I am in misalignment, or in my shame, my body lets me know. My stomach pain returns. It is undeniable, and no diets or healthy eating habits have changed this fact. When I take the action I need to take in order to be true to myself, the pain disappears.

The mental, emotional, physical and spiritual connection that we experience as whole beings is crucial to holistic healing. It is very important to be aware of it and use it as another tool for healing. Very often, diseases and illnesses that show up in the body have been in the making for quite some time. It would take years of suppressed emotion, anger, fear and low self-worth to create the pain I was feeling. I had severe inflammation in my gut and it was starting to affect my other organs. This is not to say that the real, physical ailment wasn't present, it absolutely was, and still can be. It is to show that when I addressed the emotional and spiritual needs I was suppressing, the pain dissipated.

Emotional and spiritual energies get blocked in us when we are not addressing them. This is another layer of healing that can help free us and allow us to access our authenticity.

Here is an exercise that dramatically helped me relieve this pain. I use it often when discomfort shows back up, or those butterflies of anxiety return, and I can't seem to pinpoint what is going on. Listening to your body is a beautiful gift.

Practice: Focusing exercise

Is there any area of your body in which you are experiencing physical discomfort? Do you have major knee issues that don't really seem to be for any particular reason? Lower stomach pain? Back? This could include past or current discomforts. If there is not a specific area that is causing you discomfort, I suggest focusing on the solar plexus. It is our gut and upper stomach, where you would feel butterflies in your tummy.

Close your eyes and focus all your attention on that area. Take a few deep breaths and bring your attention continuously to the area holding the discomfort. If your mind or attention wanders, that's okay. Simply bring your attention back to this area when you notice your mind wandering.

Take a few deep breaths and feel the breath going into the focal point. Imagine a white light above your head that is going to go through the top of your head. Draw the white light slowly down through your body and into the focal point. This white light will shine truth on to the shadow being held in this spot. When the light shines on to it, what do you see? If you don't see anything, is it trying to tell you something? Is there a visual image, a colour, a feeling? Ask the discomfort what it is trying to tell you.

Sit in this space of questioning and curiosity for as long as you need.

When you feel you have gained as much information as you can from the pain, imagine the white light is going through and picking up all of the darkness, putting it into a ball. It is wrapping the ball with white light. When you have unveiled all the nooks and crannies and everything that can be has been overturned right now, begin pulling this ball through your body with the white light, slowly back up through the top of your head. Release it to your higher self and the universe. Envision it moving like a balloon into the sky until you can no longer see it. The universe is taking care of it.

Open your eyes.

Pull out your journal and write down as much information as you can from this meditation. What did you find out? What did the pain tell you? Include as much detail as you can. This process can unveil some inner knowledge that was not in your awareness. It can be a really beautiful and telling process. Get in touch with what you discovered and use this new awareness to move forward.

Shadow

Everyone is a moon and has a dark side which he never shows to anyone.
– Mark Twain

A major component of our shame comes from our shadow. It is intertwined and there are different aspects to it. Carl Jung described the shadow as "the negative side of the personality, the sum of all those unpleasant qualities we like to hide, together with the insufficiently developed functions and content of the personal unconscious."

The shadow is, ultimately, the parts of ourselves that we have learned to recognize as darkness. We have been taught that darkness is bad and we therefore repress it. We are taught what is good and bad as children, and the parts of us that are seen as bad we store in the shadow. Then, they remain there. They are parts of us that we unconsciously (or sometimes, even consciously) decide that we do not want. That if we show these parts of ourselves, we will not be loved. Nobody will want us. Our connection and attachment needs will not be met.

The problem with repressing our shadow is that we are all inherently made up of light and dark, positive and negative emotions and qualities. We have all done, said or felt things we wish we hadn't. These experiences, along with our shame, make up the shadow. They don't ever go anywhere unless we address them, honour them and release what needs to be released. Honesty is a big piece of shadow work. I feel it is necessary to touch upon these components of ourselves to help us release some of our blocks. We can incorporate the dark and the light, as we need both in order to be balanced, whole people.

What is crucial to recognize about the shadow, and our perception of light and dark, good and bad, is that it is just that, a perception. None of these traits is bad or good, they are just perceived that way. It is our thoughts around the emotions or actions that we don't feel good about that turn into the shadow. When we speak to them, we can recognize and accept that rather than being negative, they can just *be*. Some of our major blocks come from these pieces. We need to be courageous and address them in order to access our authentic selves.

If we don't address our darkness? It will continue to remain in control.

The Disowned Self

The disowned self is the part of us that we pretend does not exist. The shadow contains our repressed anger that we were told was a bad emotion to express, our grief, which we were told not to show, and our secrets, the actions we took when we were misaligned with authenticity, and therefore we carry guilt and shame about. These disowned qualities aren't bad qualities, but we have been taught that they are bad. So, we push them down, we bury them deep. Part of letting the light into the shadow is honouring the parts of ourselves that we have forgotten, repressed or essentially tried to pretend did not exist. They get pushed into our unconsciousness and are not easily accessible.

I am not sure when it happened, but at some point in my life, I repressed my creativity. I believe it started in middle school and continued through high school, but I continued to repress every part of me that was "creative" and not "intellectual." There wasn't one major instance that led to this, there were a few. Somewhere along the way, I believed I was not good enough artistically and creatively to show that piece of me to the world, so I pretended it did not exist. It did not happen consciously, but years later, I look back and I know that it happened.

I used to love to draw, write, play music and dance. I was never incredible at any of them, but I loved it. I believe a series of small rejections surrounding the arts led me to believe that I would not be loved or accepted if I continued down that path, so I stopped.

Creativity is a beautiful, essential part of our existence. Creativity can show up in myriad ways for everyone, but creative expression is a core need. I rejected this. I said, "Nope, I won't be cool or loved or popular if I do that," so I stopped. Creativity was then stored in my shadow. It did not go anywhere, and shame allowed it to stay there for a really long time. There is absolutely nothing wrong with creativity; in fact, just the opposite. But, it was part of my shadow, the part of me I buried at that point in time. It became part of my disowned self.

There are two important qualities that are typically in the disowned self for most people in our culture. They are our vulnerability – as it is seen as weakness and we have been told to hide it – and our sensitivity.

A big thing to note about the shadow is that the intention is not to get rid of it. It is to honour it, to acknowledge that we see it, to be honest about what it is and how it can show up for us. If we are honest and release fear around the shadow, it does not have the power to control us. By being judgmental around how we are feeling, we will perpetuate the cycle. We can become aware of areas of shame and shadow, without judgment, and gently release them.

If I was not willing to take a look at the disowned parts of myself, I would have never reclaimed my creativity. There is a lot of other stuff in my shadow that rears its head sometimes and I need to address it, but that is all part of the process. I am not afraid of what I might find anymore because I trust that underneath it all, my authentic self is carrying me through.

The Denied Self

A great paradox of it all is that we cannot recognize something in someone else that we do not have within us. If someone is lying, and we recognize it, it is because somewhere in us, we have the capability to lie. We typically judge this part of someone else, as we have denied its existence within us. If someone is rude and it disturbs us, it is because we have been rude in the past and suppressed it. There might be more to the situation and it is yours to get curious about, to get curious about what is behind it and what parts of us are being addressed. But, part of it will be the shadow. This is when the shadow controls us – when it pins us against others. Then, it can hinder our humanity, compassion and connection with others.

It is important to remember that none of this is actually negative, it is our perception of these inherent aspects that creates the negativity. Although the shadow contains darkness, we need darkness in order to be whole; we need the darkness to balance out the light. The darkness doesn't have to be bad. If we shine light on it, we can integrate the dark and the light into one whole.

Get curious:

1.Awareness

What characteristics do you admire in others? What do you wish you had more of?

What characteristics do you find repulsive in others? What traits create a physical response in you? Write them all down. Write down a time when you exemplified these qualities.

The reality is that we can't recognize pieces of others that we don't have in ourselves. Recognizing each and every piece of ourselves is the key to healing the shadow.

2. Acceptance

Use the focusing exercise from earlier in this chapter. Bring in the light.

Accept these pieces as components of your unhealed self, but not pieces of who you really are.

3. Action

Release. Write everything down, and release. See Chapter 5 on letting go for other releasing rituals.

4. Healing

The "Just Like Me Tool":

Practice: Just Like Me

My friend shared a great tool for honouring the parts of us that are still unconscious:

Next time someone is fumbling with their purse in line at the grocery store, and you are impatient and pissed off, say to yourself, "I have been there, I have been that person, they are Just Like Me."

When someone cuts you off driving and your default is to swear, speed up and say something to them at the next light, try saying, "I have done that before, too, we all make mistakes and they are Just Like Me."

Our shame wants to keep us separate, *apart from*. It is a defence mechanism so we don't get hurt or an attempt to get our needs met, but it is a faulty one. The shadow, shame and disowned parts of us are a natural process, a biological, instinctual process that is not a result of anybody else, but our human instinct to protect ourselves.

The problem is, we need connection. We need to see ourselves as on this journey together. If we can honour the shame in us, and in turn, honour it in someone else – honour their shadow, honour where they have made mistakes – we will be able to transform our own lives in miraculous ways and ripple this grace through the world.

So next time someone around you makes a mistake, release them from their shame by demonstrating love and compassion. You will not regret acting out of love, because it will honour the darkness in you, too.

- Seven-
<u>The Second Layer:</u>
Core Beliefs and Fears

Self-worth comes from one thing: thinking that you are worthy.
– Wayne Dyer

A solid mixture of authenticity, messages we received as children and shame create our core beliefs. Our core beliefs are not only a layer in themselves but are also mixed in amongst the other layers and help to develop each of them. Our core beliefs are a huge part of how we operate in the world, positively or negatively.

Our core beliefs are where our sense of worthiness come from. If we truly believe we are worthy of love, affection, success, happiness, joy, whatever we need, this comes from a core belief that we are worthy of receiving the amazing gifts life has to offer. If we believe at our core that we are not good enough, that we do not deserve joy and peace, or that we don't deserve the job we so desperately want, or the girlfriend who seems way out of our league, we will not see these gifts manifest. Our core beliefs dictate so much of our lives and how we operate in the world, and they are an essential layer to look at along this journey.

I am going to share a positive and a negative core belief that I have always had, and that have sort of conflicted with each other my whole life.

Positive

The first core belief is that I can do whatever I want to do in life, and I can be whoever I want to be. As long as I work hard and set my mind to it, I can do anything. I have this incredible core belief instilled in me from my dad. There has never been a point in my life when I have actually felt that I have barriers in front of me in terms of career development, education and "what I want to be when I grow up." I genuinely have believed my entire life that the world is my oyster and I can have any job, go to any school or have any life I choose. I am beyond grateful for this core belief. It is one of the reasons I am chasing my dreams today.

Negative

The second, and quite contradictory, core belief that has come into my awareness is that I am a world-class screw up. I blame myself for everything. Sorry, Mom, but I learned this one from you!

The year I was living in Seoul, I wasn't able to make it home for Christmas. Peter came over to visit me for the holidays and we went on an adventure together. We travelled to Thailand, Vietnam and Malaysia. It was amazing, but I had my fair share of crazy, insecure moments. These typically stemmed from something happening that was well beyond my control, like the weather quickly turning from sun to rain, or a line-up at customs, or ridiculous traffic.

I would take on these problems as if I had some sort of responsibility for them. I put so much pressure on myself to plan the perfect trip with my boyfriend, who I wasn't going to see again for six months, that I believed every little thing that went wrong would ruin our trip and be my fault.

Ok, so, first issue: this is insanely self-centred thinking. As if the traffic in Bangkok has anything to do with me! However, I took it on. I thought that if I had made the decision to take the train instead of a cab, and seeing more of the city that way, we would get to our hotel faster and things would be so much easier. Peter, I might add, was totally fine. Going with the flow, he didn't flinch at the traffic. Meanwhile, I was having a nervous breakdown over it.

The point is, I have this core belief that I should be able to fix things, and if I can't, there is something wrong with me. I have taken on so many situations that are out of my control due to this belief, as I'm sure you realize by now.

These beliefs have manifested in so many different ways in my life. What's different now is my perspective on them, through awareness. So much of this book is about bringing our shadows into light, and this is one of them. Admitting this *sucks*. Admitting that I can still go into crazy-girl thinking is tough. But, it can heal me and hopefully, it can help you in your healing journey too.

Writing Your Myth:
Another way of framing core beliefs is by using the term "myth." A myth is, by definition, a widely held but false belief or idea. What myths have you been telling yourself your entire life? If you were to write your story right now, what themes would emerge, and what would your perspective on those themes be? Would they be the same as someone else's?

Take 20 minutes and use this as a journal prompt. What core beliefs have been dictating so much of your life?

Moving Through Fear

Fear is the cheapest room in the house. I'd like to see you in better living conditions.
— Hafez of Persia

Every moment of every day we have a choice: to choose love or fear.

I speak about fear throughout the entire book. It is important, and it tells us so much. When I am acting in a way that is in misalignment with authenticity, the reason always comes down to fear. When I am acting from a sub-personality, a defence or through an addiction, I am operating out of fear. Aligning with our authentic selves gives us the choice to act out of love, for ourselves and others.

Some of my biggest fears:

- Fear of not being enough
- Fear of not having enough
- Fear of judgment or criticism
- Fear of confrontation
- Fear of intimacy
- Fear of attachment
- Fear of being happy
- Fear of the unknown
- Fear of change
- Fear of becoming a burden
- Fear of success
- Fear of failure

- Fear of rejection
- Fear of lack of control
- Fear of vulnerability
- Fear of death

Some of the inauthentic needs driving these fears include:

- The need to know
- The need to be right
- The need to get even
- The need to look good
- The need to judge
- The need to keep score
- The need to control

I will go through phases where things are going really well in my life and I am extremely happy. At work I will feel fulfilled with my emotional connections and balanced with my personal time. Usually, when this happens, I begin to move into a mode of fear, also known as freaking out and self-sabotaging.

I have a huge fear of letting myself be happy. Because when I do, it doesn't stay that way. So, I try to control the situation by preparing myself for the inevitable shoe to drop. Except this just removes my happiness in that moment and takes me out of being present. I move into a state of anxiety, as I am worrying about the future.

Several times throughout our relationship, Peter would answer the phone in a less-than-enthusiastic way and I would instantly accuse him of being high. An off-moment for him would create an obsession cycle for me and cause huge paranoia and fear. Why would an off-moment terrify me to my core and throw me into an obsession cycle where I was willing to sabotage my happiness and peace in an instant? I was triggered by my old trauma around his relapses.

A trigger on a gun is such a small piece of the gun itself. There is so much more to it – the ammunition, the barrel… Well, I know absolutely nothing about guns, but I know that the trigger is small! The point is, the trigger is what launches everything else, but the trigger would be nothing without the other components of the gun. The trigger can't work on its own.

When Peter would answer the phone this way or look tired or awkward during a FaceTime call, I would be triggered. I would see flashes of old behaviour and it would bring up a lot of stuff that I had thought I had healed.

However, I began to realize that I had been having these fears come up a lot lately, and I was pushing them away. I was telling myself that everything was fine, and I was being paranoid. However, that is not the way to actually move through the fear, as it suppresses how you are actually feeling. Suppressing fear does nothing but ensure it will come out in some way, shape or form later on. In trying to pretend some of these fears just weren't happening, they ended up inevitably being triggered.

I had been so happy that I was becoming fearful. It sounds contradictory, but that is the way that I operate. If everything is going well, what happens when it doesn't? I don't want to experience that pain again, so I am going to brace myself or find something right now that tells me everything isn't alright, because then I will be in control and if I am in control, everything will be fine. This is inauthentic thinking, and fear, the controller and my inner saboteur have taken over.

What I have learned? That I have to move through the fear. I have to honour what I am feeling in each and every moment. I can't pretend it isn't happening. I can't wish fear away. I can pray for help in moving through it. I can choose to act out of love to help move through it. But I cannot pretend it isn't happening.

Get curious:

How I dealt with a specific experience of being triggered:

1. Awareness
I was triggered. I had to become aware of the trigger and of my physical, emotional and mental response to that trigger. I had to become aware of all the behaviours that were involved, and get honest about the fears that were underlying my quick shift in thinking.

2. Acceptance
In accepting the moment for how it really was, I regained the power of choice. I regained the power to choose a healthier thought or to believe everything was okay. I knew I was in fear. I asked Peter if he was okay. He could tell I was triggered. He assured me that everything was fine. I believed him, but I was still in fear. I told him I needed a few minutes and hopped off the call to put my acceptance into action.

3. Action
a) I prayed. I got on my knees and prayed. I prayed for the universe to help me through this fear, and for my authentic self to come into alignment. I asked for acceptance, I asked to be present, to help me honour what I have been through and to acknowledge that it will take some time for all the wounds to be healed. I felt instantly better.

b) I set a boundary. I called Peter back, and I was tearing up. I told him I was in a lot of fear and that I knew it had nothing to do with him. He asked what he could do to help, and I asked if he could help me maintain a boundary where he speaks to someone else about any thoughts he might have about using, and not me. That I needed to trust he was speaking to other people. That I could not control his thoughts or his processes, and I needed that space in order to continue healing the trauma of his relapse. He said he thought that was a good idea, and he would share with someone else.

d) I decided to choose love over fear. And continued to do it over and over, until it stuck. I chose to bombard the fearful thought with positive thoughts, to reinforce that things are okay and exactly as they needed to be in this moment.

c) I talked it through. Our dialogue went like this from then on: I am afraid of being happy and everything falling apart again. I am afraid of letting myself be vulnerable or saying that I am okay out loud so that I don't look or feel stupid if it doesn't work out. I am afraid to plan for our future because I planned for our future before and it didn't go the way I planned. I am afraid of my feelings and I don't want to be in pain, so I have been pretending that I haven't had these thoughts or feelings of fear at all, but I have. I need to acknowledge them so that they cannot control me. I need to feel the fear and take the loving action anyways.

I said thank you to the universe for having my back, and to Peter for listening to me, and I wrote down what I was grateful for: a loving and supportive relationship, the ability to recognize my own shit now and a safe home to fall apart in.

4. Healing

When I look back on all of this, the fears were so real at the time, and when I chose love over fear, I could move through them. What I am realizing more often than not is that change is one of my biggest fears, but it is the inevitability of life. We are changing every moment of every day. And, if you are reading this book, you are open to your life changing in so many wonderful ways. I sure am. But, I fear those changes. I cling to the old version of myself and have a hard time letting go of that person. In aligning with the universe and my authentic self, I can flow with change and allow it to come, as it is going to anyways. Rather than focusing on the situation or attaching to the fear, I can choose love. I can trust the universe and my truth and ride out the shifts. The view from the top of that mountain is always beautiful.

Practice: Moving Through Fear

Prayer

It has been said that prayer is how we ask, and meditation is how we receive. This is true for me, and although usually prayer and meditation are coupled together, they look very different. Prayer allows me to choose love over fear the moment I wake up, and meditation allows me to come back to that choice throughout the day by aligning with universal guidance.

This journey back to authenticity will have you challenge some of your core belief systems and become open to new ways of thinking. To heal holistically means being open to spirituality as well.

In that, prayer is an important part of surrender. It is releasing to the universe what we cannot control or aspects and character traits that are no longer serving us. There is no shame in believing in something bigger. Relying on something bigger is humbling, accepting, courageous. And it makes you vulnerable. It is a profound source of strength.

For me, the word "God" was always very triggering. I never had a bad relationship with religion, but somewhere along the line, it just didn't match up for me anymore. What I began to gain faith in was the positive stories I heard of other women changing their lives. When I heard of women who had been through what I had been through and actually changed and were living these beautiful, happy and free lives, I had a bit of faith that I could do the same thing. When I opened up to the possibility that there was something bigger than me at work in the world, I opened the door to faith. When that door was open, I began to experience synchronicities and notice moments that felt divinely guided. With those awarenesses, my faith grew. With every experience that seemed divinely guided, such as the ability I was gaining to make the changes in my life that I never could have made on my own, my faith grew. When I moved through so much pain I never thought I would pick myself up again, my faith grew.

My favourite prayer, and where I started, is by saying, "Please help me choose love over fear today," and right before going to bed, saying thank you. I look up into sky (or ceiling) when I open my eyes in the morning, say my gratitude list, and then I ask for help in choosing love over fear, and I say thank you. It is the last thing I do before falling asleep at night, as well. Now, my prayers have deepened, but they always involve me surrendering what I think needs to be to what my authentic self and the universe knows is best for me.

Give it a try. Challenge yourself to open up to possibilities. Challenge yourself to choose love over fear. Ask Mother Nature, the spirit of the universe, God, your higher self or your authentic self for help, each and every day. Start to feel the surrender and release of allowing life to happen the way it is meant to, and start trusting the journey. Your authentic self has your back and will carry you through if you let it.

Remind yourself to continue being gentle, kind and loving towards yourself throughout this journey. It can be painful and revealing, and you are being vulnerable and brave in being willing to look at these layers and blocks. Authentic living is not always easy, but it is worth it. You will live your best life if you live in your truth. There is freedom on the other side. Just remember to always seek outside help if you need it throughout the process or reach out to people you trust. Keep a journal, highlight what resonates deeply and share the love. The world needs you, living in your truth.

Cultivating an Attitude of Gratitude

Gratitude makes sense if our past, brings peace for today, and creates a vision for tomorrow.

- *Melody Beattie*

Okay, #grateful has been trending on Instagram for a while now, and I am all for it. It is a quick way to come into the present moment, release negative thoughts, feelings and emotions, and shift our behaviour. Gratitude has changed my life and is a crucial component in authentic living.

I was about two weeks sober. I was calling my friend Shelly, who I met at Canyon Ranch, incessantly. I felt like a child with no direction. I literally called her to help me decide if I should order coffee or tea from Starbucks. Our conversations were typically of me gabbing on about how incredible life was and about all of the beautiful things that I was noticing that I had been blind to before. Early in recovery this phenomenon is called the "pink cloud," where the natural high seems better than the high you were getting from the alcohol or drugs.

However, on this particular day, I was pretty angry. I was experiencing my strongest craving to drink since putting it down for good and I was resentful as all hell that I couldn't indulge. It was the second week of July, a Saturday afternoon. I was walking down Bloor Street in Toronto and everyone was enjoying patio beers. I wanted to join in. After all, that was my absolute favourite pastime – daytime drinking on a patio (or anywhere, really). There was nothing better, or so I thought. I was pissed off to say the least. I was using the tools Shelly had suggested, like "playing the tape to the end," which basically means that if I view my life like a movie and watch through, what will happen if I pick up that first drink? Inevitably, I will destroy my life and I don't know when I will be able to stop drinking again. I kept playing the tape, but it wasn't enough. I was told that if I was ever craving a drink or struggling with my thoughts, I needed to pick up the phone and call Shelly, not pick up a drink. Since my failed judgment had got me to where I was, I listened to this advice.

So, I called her. I was bitching and moaning about how I am never going to be able to drink on a patio and it's so nice and it's not fair and why me? Life wasn't fair! I wanted to be drinking on a patio. It wasn't fair. And so on, and so forth, and whining some more, until she finally cut me off. She said, "I hear you, but let's try something else. You're going to text me 20 things you're grateful for right now." And then she hung up. Um, hello? I mean, if I was angry before, I was raging now.

That being said, Shelly had not steered me wrong thus far, so I resentfully opened up a message to her on my phone and started writing the list: my parents, my dog, the beautiful weather, finally sleeping at night again, not feeling nauseous, feeling healthy, feeling honest, the new friends I was making… Around this point, something shifted. I felt light. I felt… happy? I couldn't figure out what had just happened. My mood and mind and energy shifted so fast. I wasn't sure what it was, but I knew something big had just happened. I finished the list and by the end, everything was different.

I was grateful. I truly understood what this meant for the first time in my life. To appreciate everything around me and to recognize all of life's gifts, not just the bad, the unfairness, the negative. I had always had such a beautiful life, but the layers of blockage I was experiencing were not allowing me to truly feel it, and my unhealthy behaviours were running the show. For the first time, everything clicked for me. My mindset needed to shift; my thoughts really can control everything. Maybe actually listening to what other people have suggested based on their successful experiences would also give me the ability to profoundly change my own life.

It was in this moment that the obsession to drink left me. I felt it leave my body and it has not returned since. I realized right then and there that if I was to go back to how I had been living, and not stayed on this path I had begun to trudge down, I would lose all the things I just listed that I was grateful for. I needed to recognize and be grateful for what I did have, rather than focusing on the lack. I needed to focus on all the gifts that I would lose if I continued down this self-destructive path. I needed to take responsibility, and although some things had happened to me throughout my life that I couldn't control or change, I could change my life now. As I write this, I have tears running down my cheeks. Every time I edit this book and read this chapter, I cry. Because that's how beautiful and opening this moment was for me. To say I am grateful would be the most profound understatement I could give. But grateful is the best word to describe it. I have made daily gratitude lists since this moment, and I urge all of you to try it out.

I describe gratitude now as a shift in emotional, mental and physical being from that of lack to that of acceptance. Gratitude is the experience of a profound thankfulness for each and every moment, encounter and person in our lives. It is a reminder of all the good in this world. There is always something to be grateful for, even in the darkest of hours.

And that is when I need it the most – when I am feeling low. In maintaining gratitude, I can build it up when I am feeling good and use it as a defence against my negative thoughts. That way, when I am low, the low doesn't feel so low. Rather than reminding myself that this amazing moment will pass, as I inevitably will soon have a moment of impatience, judgment or resentment come up, I continuously make cultivating an attitude of gratitude a priority in my life. First thing in the morning, I say three things I am grateful for. I do the same at night. This can be written, but sometimes just spoken, depending on the day, but now it comes as naturally as breathing. It comes the moment I open my eyes in the morning, because I make it a priority. I use this tool throughout the day if I need to, particularly when icky feelings are coming up. It quickly shifts my thinking and I can go on with my day with a little more peace. I encourage you to adopt this practice. It is one of the single most important practices in my life today.

Practice: Gratitude Lists

A great way to start is to pull out a pen and paper now. Write down as many things as you can think of that you are grateful for. Sometimes, this can be the pillow under your head, a hot meal or a glass of water. Sometimes, it can be your partner or children or friend. Sometimes, it can be a home, knowing so many people are not so fortunate to have a roof over their heads. It is a reminder of how blessed we are, and we are so very blessed.

Now, try writing three to five, or more, things you are grateful for, starting right now, and every morning and evening for the next week.

Notice the feelings that shift or emotions that come up. It is all a part of the awareness and acceptance process. How have things shifted this week as a result of this practice? Have they shifted at all? How did it feel emotionally? Mentally? Physically? I know there is a pit in my stomach that can be easily relieved through gratitude, so maybe there is a physical shift that occurs for you too. Notice everything and anything that comes up. Get curious about those shifts and new awarenesses.

- Eight -
The Third Layer:
False Selves

It takes courage to grow up and become who you really are.
– E.E. Cummings

Our false selves develop from core beliefs and fears that our needs will not be met, particularly our need for connection and authenticity. Why does our personality change at different times in our lives, or depending on the people we are with and how we are behaving? Because it is not really who we are.

We typically develop sub-personalities as children as a form of protection when we are vulnerable. As shame is the first layer that is protecting our essence from being hurt, sub-personalities form on top of shame and are primarily fear-based. These sub-personalities or "false selves" can take over at times. They all have different methods of getting their needs met and are inauthentic pieces of ourselves that we may actually describe as our personality. They benefit us and are learned ways to get these needs met… until they don't. At some point, they will stop working for us.

False selves are built on layers of shame and are a culmination of our thoughts, feelings and actions. They are learned behaviours, ways we are trying to get our connection and authenticity needs met, and are ultimately an attempt at validation, security and control. They are the parts of our personalities that come in extremes, and as they are completely able to run the show for us, they are a huge block to authentic living.

Part of the journey into authenticity is recognizing these sub-personalities and how they manifest in us. But, not only do we want to recognize them, we want to release the unhealthy pieces of them and merge them into our whole self, in a balanced and healthy way. This is not a judgment against our false selves and it is not a combative approach in any way. It is to recognize that they have served a purpose for us, came into being for a reason, for core needs and survival, and although they may no longer be serving us, they may have helped us along the way. The problem is that when we are so detached from authenticity, these false selves can become quite dissociated and take on a life of their own.

There are healthy balances to every personality trait we have. We can be free-spirited, help out our friends in need by being of service, be witty and funny and work really hard at what we do. The false selves are extreme versions of these personality traits. They turn into defects. They become unhealthy and ultimately destructive. They have been formed to meet unhealthy needs, but we can transform them into healthy personality traits.

Common False Selves

The Perfectionist

The perfectionist is a huge sub-personality for so many people I know. I definitely have it. The perfectionist tells us that if we are not perfect, we are not loveable. It believes that we are so deeply flawed and damaged that we need to present ourselves perfectly to the world or our core connection needs will not be met. This thinking and behaviour pattern will lead to anxiety, depression and addiction, as it is impossible for anybody in this world to be perfect all the time. Our essence is perfect and pure, but we are human, and that means we are dramatically imperfect.

In order to shift the perfectionist sub-personality, it is important to recognize the underlying fears of rejection and failure that are beneath this false self. What if you weren't perfect? What would happen? Get curious around where perfectionism pops up for you, and journal on what is underneath it.

The All-or-Nothing Thinker

The all-or-nothing thinker usually goes hand in hand with the perfectionist. This sub-personality thrives on black-or-white thinking and hates living in any area of grey. Grey is unknown and murky, and this is too overwhelming for this false self. Thinking in all-or-nothing terms leaves no room for error. It keeps us safe.

The problem is that, as we know, life doesn't operate in black and white. All-or-nothing thinking creates distortions and oppositions within us. We are either an entire success or an utter failure. We are happy and joyous, or miserable and depressed. Everything is extreme and polarizing. By noticing when we are having all-or-nothing thinking patterns, we can begin to shift this area and live in the grey.

The Controller

I speak about the controller throughout this book in a variety of different ways. It develops from our core need for security and a fear and mistrust of the universe. The controller feels very out of control, so over-controls the things that they can. The problem is that the only thing we actually have control over is ourselves and our core needs will not be met by trying to control other people's lives. My controller was evidently active through so many of my experiences and is still one false self I need to consistently acknowledge and release.

The Overachiever

One of my most prevalent false selves is the overachiever. I have spent my entire life trying to achieve academically in order to gain the approval I so desperately seek. I never felt good enough and the instant approval I felt when I did well in school, became captain of a sports team or got the job I didn't feel good enough for satisfied my need for external validation and instant approval. The problem with this is that it never authentically satisfies the sense of unworthiness that I feel. I will never have enough approval, and I will gain to seek it in other, more unhealthy ways. This false self was one that turned into an addiction for me, a workaholic overachiever when it came to academia and, when that didn't work, I turned to alcohol.

The Strong One

Another one I struggle with is being the pillar of strength. It is just a façade and I need love and support as much as anyone else. I was always so terrified of being vulnerable that if I put on a brave face and sucked it up, I wouldn't be seen as weak. The problem is that it is so terrifying for me to ask for help that I tried for years to manage everything on my own. Ultimately, this failed, and I was forced into surrendering and humbling myself to a point of being willing to ask for help. When people deem you as being strong they sometimes won't offer help. By being in touch with our core needs and not our false, shame-based needs, we can ask for help and allow ourselves to be vulnerable, and that takes more bravery than anything.

The People-Pleaser

The people-pleaser meets their inauthentic attachment needs by over-doing it for other people. They are not in touch with their own needs, or they dismiss them in order to fulfil the needs of others. They don't feel worthy of having boundaries and feel they can only get the love they deserve if they bend over backwards for others.

I had such a blind spot when it came to my people-pleasing. I did not realize how much of a people-pleaser I was until I came into recovery. The overachiever, I was super aware of. The people-pleaser was buried in my subconscious. When I did an inventory of my resentments, I realized that an enormous amount came from people-pleasing. I was mad when someone took advantage of me, I never set boundaries and it got me into a lot of trouble. I told people what they wanted to hear so that they would like me. I put myself in compromising situations because I was fearful of confrontation. I over-exerted myself in every way out of fear they wouldn't love me.

Boundaries are the antidote for people-pleasing. Saying no can be so difficult, and looking at the underlying shame-based fears behind people-pleasing will help shift the need to live for others and allow us to begin living for ourselves.

The Caretaker

The caretaker puts the needs of others above themselves. They believe they can fix everything and everyone, and everything will be okay if they are taking care of the situation. Their core fears are typically rejection and abandonment. They believe that if they are taking care of others, those people won't be able to leave them. They surround themselves with people who are reliant on them (usually in their addict or victim sub-personalities) so that they don't have to take a look at themselves. I was a huge, resentful, caretaker. I would run to save other people at the expense of my own boundaries. I did this in relationships, friendships and with my family. I would drop everything if somebody needed me. I could fix it. I could find the magic words that would make it better. Some things are just out of our control and that was a hard pill for me to swallow. I took care of people for a long time and became very resentful when my need for love wasn't returned.

The Victim

The victim believes life is happening *to* them and feels out of control of their situation. It is a defence mechanism to avoid the fear of change, fear of failure or fear of success. The core addiction behind the victim sub-personality is suffering. It can be out of a fear of the unknown and a fear of unworthiness. They can go into the "why me" and believe that everything bad that has ever happened is happening to them. They sit in their suffering and believe there is nothing they can do to change their situation.

I didn't know how terribly I fell into this false self until a recent hard look in the mirror. I didn't want to make the changes necessary out of fear, and so I continued to let the weight of the world fall on my shoulders. By releasing toxic relationships, unhealthy thinking and really digging into some fear and shame, I was able to begin looking at what I was gaining out of being in victim mode.

The Critic

The critic does just what it says, criticizes. Everything and everyone. They are most critical of themselves, however, but they might outwardly try and control your perception of them by criticizing you or someone else. They are afraid of being seen, as they are in their shame of not being good enough. They have severely negative self-talk and that is put out into the world. The critic tries to put up a wall out of fear of vulnerability. Everyone has an inner critic, and the critic sub-personality is an extreme version of this. Our inner critic can help us in some ways, but this critic takes things too far.

The Clown

We all know a clown – someone who is afraid of being vulnerable, so they actually put themselves out there comically so you cannot see the fears going on behind the scenes. They are afraid that they won't be loved if they are themselves. This doesn't mean that being funny is a negative sub-personality. The clown is an extreme, shame-based version of this characteristic. It is a need for external approval and validation because they do not feel loveable without this shield.

The Free Spirit

The free spirit appears carefree and resilient. They "go with the flow." This personality is based on a fear of commitment, fear of failure and a fear of vulnerability. The free spirit doesn't want to be tied down, which develops from a fear of not wanting to be seen for who they really are. I go into this mode of escape when things get tough for me.

The Partier

Need to be the centre of attention? Always the girl standing on the furniture, dancing on the bar or doing body shots? Yeah, that was me. I needed to be the centre of attention when I went out. I needed the external validation. I needed to be seen. However, I also needed to be protected while being seen. You couldn't see me for who I really was because that was someone you wouldn't like. So, I became the life of the party. Everyone will always want her around, right? The healing piece for the partier false-self is intimacy, real connection. That needs to start with getting to know ourselves a little bit better.

Get curious:

1. Awareness
Which false-self traits stand out to you immediately? Where have you been resentful in your life that could be an indicator of a false self? What fears are behind those traits? Refer to the fears list on page 78.

2. Acceptance
You cannot do better if you don't know better. Accept that these traits helped you for a time, or they wouldn't have been developed in the first place.

3. Action
Set boundaries and be honest about what your needs really are. It is okay to ask someone to help you meet your authentic needs. Let's look at how to get clear on what our boundaries are and how

---

to set them. This step ensures that you remain aligned with your authenticity, rather than relying on an old pattern and false self. Remember to be willing to show your vulnerability and have faith.

4. Healing

The more consistent we are in living an authentic life the faster our false selves will heal. Time takes time and be gentle with yourself and follow the first three steps again if a false self appears to be taking over.

Priorities, Boundaries, and our False Selves

Priorities

Priorities are an excellent way to shift the mindset from scarcity to abundance (see Chapter 10), from not having enough time to focusing our time on what is really important, to really, truly put yourself, your needs and your desires at the forefront of your life. There is a difference between being selfish and being self-centred, and being selfish can be a really positive and necessary quality. You are your own advocate, you have the ability and power to design your own life. It is time to make *you* a priority!

First, it is necessary to look at our relationship with time. I have always had a pretty scarce view of time. My first thought in the morning is, "I didn't sleep enough," or "There isn't enough time to get all of my work done today." Now, I have shifted my relationship with time to reflect my priorities. If I don't feel I have time to have dinner with a friend, I will say that I actually need to because it's important to me. Deepak Chopra says that time is the great equalizer. Everyone has 24 hours in a day, regardless of whether you are the Queen of England, Bill Gates or a barista in your favourite coffee shop.

When shifting our language around time, we can come to realize what is really important to us. Try it out. Some of my dialogue around time scarcity:

- I cannot go to the gym, I don't have time.

- I cannot make my meals, I don't have time.

- I cannot meet up with my friend, I don't have time.

Now try it this way:

- I cannot go to the gym because working out is not a priority for me.

- I cannot make my own meals because eating healthily is not a priority for me.

- I cannot meet my friend because that friendship is not a priority for me.

See what happens? I realized by shifting this language that I was not taking enough time for what is really best for me. I was not present, I was not mindful, and I was definitely not prioritizing my needs. There is always time for what we prioritize. What I was prioritizing was not what I authentically needed. I need to prioritize my health and wellness, my connections and the work that I find fulfilling. That means letting go of the guilt, shame and fears I have around saying no and putting myself first. Prioritizing ourselves engages our worthiness and allows our mind, body and spirit to trust that we are taking care of ourselves.

Some of my all-time favourite, mind-shifting questions that help determine where my needs really are and make me a priority are:

What is the most loving thing you can do, for you? This really shifts my thinking, fast. Sometimes, the most loving thing I can do is turn off the computer, stop working and watch a movie. Sometimes, it is waking up early and working out. Sometimes, it is saying no to the cake that will make me feel like garbage. Sometimes, it's indulging in the ice cream. Whatever it is, if I ask myself, "What is the most loving thing for me, right now?" it cuts right through my shame, right through my thinking and rationalizing, and gets to my truth. I can then make the next right decision, for me.

What is something your future self will thank you for? My future self is not going to thank me if I am exhausted because my people-pleaser insisted I go to a party the night before when everything in me was screaming not to. My future self is not going to thank me for yelling at a co-worker and having to apologize later for it. My future self will not thank me if I eat so many tacos for dinner that my stomach hurts.

What my future self will always thank me for is if I authentically do the right thing for myself, in that moment. If I don't finish a paper because I actually really need to catch up on sleep, my future self will be happy I am well rested. If I am being complacent or fearful and not finishing work because of that, my future self will feel stressed about that decision. Again, this question helps cut right to the core of what we really need in that moment.

What do you really want? What do you really need? Sometimes, I need to stop and be clear about what my needs really are in a situation. Do I need to go out and connect with some friends, or do I need to stay home and have a self-care night in? Do I need to sleep for another hour, or do I need to get my butt up and get to yoga? Do I really actually want to be friends with that person? Do I feel authentic and fulfilled from it, or am I still hanging on to it because we have been friends for a long time? What do I really need?

Get clear on where your needs, desires and fulfilment lie. This will help you be able to set your priorities, get honest and cut through the shame. It will help you then become clear on what your boundaries really are and become more confident in setting them.

In order to be clear about what boundaries need to be set, you need to be clear on your priorities first.

Boundaries

There is not one person I know who does not, or has not, struggled with boundaries. Whether it is being aware that there are boundary issues to begin with, or the struggle is in maintaining boundaries, they are super tough.

Depending on what your most prominent false selves are, boundaries will come into your life in different ways. For me, whose prominent false selves are the people-pleaser, caretaker, addict, overachiever and controller, boundaries were basically non-existent in my life. I didn't know what they were, and I definitely didn't know how to enforce them. They made me dramatically uncomfortable. When I came into sobriety, I realized that a huge amount of resentments I was hanging on to were due to the lack of boundaries I had. This wasn't anybody else's responsibility but my own to become aware of and enforce. Usually, a lack of boundaries stem from childhood and shifts depending on relationships and situations. If you are really close to your family, you might have unhealthy boundaries surrounding how much you share about your life with them. If you suffered any type of abuse as a child or throughout your life, boundary struggles will absolutely be prevalent as an adult. Boundaries can be a lack of respect for yourself or stem from low self-worth. They can then shift to a lack of respect for other people's boundaries.

Unfortunately, chances are that if you aren't good at maintaining your own boundaries, you're not very good at respecting others' either.

Boundaries pop up in every area of my life and are equally challenging no matter what boundaries I am trying to set. I struggle with setting boundaries with relationships – friends, family and romantically. I have a hard time not taking on other people's emotions and making them my own. I want to fix everything for everyone, and sometimes, I don't know how to mind my own damn business. I am working on it. On the other hand, I have a hard time discerning who to talk to about certain things. This has really improved over the last few years and I know I have a few people who I am extremely close to who know the nitty-gritty details of my life. No one else needs to know my business, and with that, I need to work on my expectations of others who do not know the intimate details of my life.

I have really healed my relationship with my family through setting boundaries. It is challenging for me, as we are close, and I have positive relationships with them. However, sharing everything with them all the time opens all of us up to being hurt. I have had to learn how to discern what is appropriate to share with my mom, and what is best shared with someone else, usually my therapist.

I didn't value myself enough to have good boundaries, whether it was sexually, physically, mentally or emotionally. I used to have really bad physical boundaries with people. That is shifting now. It is hard, but once you become aware that there is a lack of boundaries, you hit a point where they need to be set.

"No" is a complete sentence

This truth was hard for me to swallow. I always felt like I needed an excuse not to do something that really didn't feel right. My people-pleaser told me that if I didn't do what you wanted me to do, you wouldn't like me. This might be true, but it's impossible to make an authentic connection this way. So, instead of making excuses, I basically said yes to everything and dealt with the consequences later. I would then be flaky on plans or lie my way out of situations because telling the truth that I just really didn't want to do something was way too scary for me. What if I said no to plans to hang out with friends and they stopped inviting me? What if I missed out on something really good? If anyone asked me to do anything for them I would bend over backwards to make it happen.

I worked through a lot of this with friends and family, but these were all beyond challenged when it came to being in a relationship with an addict. Boundaries were non-existent, once again. I couldn't enforce them, I couldn't maintain them and I certainly didn't respect them. My rationalizing defence mechanisms popped up and my need-to-know fears kicked in. There were no more boundaries for my partner, or for me.

Over time, it became apparent that boundaries were a huge issue. I couldn't justify my actions anymore. I had to start saying no, and I had to start respecting my partner. Just because he was in active addiction did not give me a right to violate his privacy, to look at his phone, to tell him what to do with his life or ask him a million questions that were none of my business. I had to start enforcing my own boundaries of not speaking to him when he was high, and when we ultimately broke up, I had to maintain my own boundaries of no communication for a good amount of time. It was excruciating, but if they are my boundaries, it is also my responsibility to maintain them. In that, make sure that your actions and your words are in alignment. It is very easy to say that we are setting a boundary but then go back on it with our actions later. Your words will not come to mean anything if your actions do not back them up, and people will unintentionally (or intentionally) take advantage of that. They will not believe what you are saying, and how can they? You aren't being really honest with yourself or them! It is hard, but it can change your life.

Eventually, setting boundaries does become easier. Life will continue to test your boundaries and once you feel like you've got a firm grasp on them, something else will pop up that you didn't even consider needed a boundary.

Set these boundaries respectfully, with compassion for the other person involved, with a firm and unwavering confidence. Even if you don't feel confident in them yet, you will. Try saying no. See how it feels. It will probably feel gut-wrenching and icky for a little while, but then it will feel empowering and freeing.

As with every change you make, you might go to an extreme at first. I certainly did. When I finally realized that I actually didn't have to do things that I didn't want to do, or that felt really wrong for me, I was addicted to saying no! I was saying no all the time, and the next problem was to balance back out and start saying yes to other things, too. It is okay, and this is how we learn and grow. Be gentle with yourself and others. Or firm, whichever feels best for you.

Try saying yes to what you really want. Help yourself to know what is really important to you. Set priorities, say yes to what fuels your soul and is healthy for you. Say no to the rest. Do *you*. Remember that other people's opinions are none of your business, and as long as you feel that you authentically set a boundary for you, the other person's response is no longer your concern.

Setting boundaries is tough. Maintaining boundaries can be even tougher. Be clear and true to you.

Get curious:

1. Awareness

What are your core values? What is most important to you? What are your priorities? These are big questions, but they are crucial in knowing where you need to set boundaries. When you become aware of these areas, you can become aware of where your lack of boundaries lies. Get clear on where boundaries have been lacking and where boundaries need to be set. Look at what the underlying fears behind the fears are. Which false self was running the show in enabling your lack of boundaries? Which fears are underlying that false self? The more aware you are of what the undercurrent of the situation is, the easier it will be to maintain the boundaries after, and the greater healing that will take place.

2. Acceptance

Be gentle with yourself that you have not set boundaries up until this point in specific areas. You didn't know better. You did the best you could. The acceptance prayer on page 28 helps me in setting boundaries with people when I feel like my controller or people-pleaser is popping up. If I am setting boundaries, the way I set them is my responsibility, and I am being true to me. Worrying about other people's reactions is natural, but their reaction is not my business. I need to keep my side of the street clean and the other person's lack of acceptance is not my responsibility. It is hard, if your major go-to sub-personality is to caretake or if you are co-dependent and take on others' emotions, but setting boundaries is a *major* step in healing your relationship with yourself, living an authentic life and actually helping others in the long run as well.

3. Action

Set your boundaries. Let someone know if something isn't okay with you. Say no when you don't want to or cannot do something or will be compromising your own values to do it. Ensure your actions are speaking to what you are saying. The more in alignment and consistent you are, the clearer and easier your boundaries will become. Maintain. Maintain. Maintain. They can be so tough, but they are so worth it. Like everything, once the habits come into place and the actions, thoughts and emotions around the situation shift, you can heal and move forward.

Being True to You

I went through a huge struggle last winter with my job in Korea. It was the middle of January, I was homesick and experiencing a heavy bout of seasonal depression. I wanted to go home to Canada. I wanted to leave so, so badly, but my gut was telling me to stay, stick it out and trust the process. Every time I felt like I had made progress and was becoming more comfortable with my work environment, things would shift. My boss started having meltdowns as the school wasn't doing as well as it once was, and this was starting to affect every aspect of the job. The problem I was experiencing with the Korean work culture is that your job is supposed to be your life, and balance isn't really in their vocabulary.

I would finally feel that I was balanced or had accepted a new shift in work and would be in a good groove for a week or so, and then I'd be thrown another curveball. I'd be clear on my priorities and boundaries and then would have to revisit them over again. So, inevitably, I was thrown another curveball. I had purchased tickets to go to the Olympics in PyeongChang for my roommate's birthday. We were going to the snowboard big air finals on the last Saturday of the two-week period.

In a teachers' meeting just a few weeks before the Olympics, we were informed that on February 24th (a Saturday, I will remind you) the kindergarten graduation was scheduled, and all the teachers needed to be there. Amelia and I were beyond pissed off at this point. We looked at each other, my boss asked what was wrong, and I told her that we had tickets to the Olympics that day. Her immediate response was that we shouldn't be booking anything more than a month in advance because that is usually the amount of time they give us notice for such events. They said something in Korean about us, a practice I had become accustomed to, and the head Korean teacher skirted out of the room. She came back and notified me that the tickets were refundable, and I would need to cancel them. I was asked to give my email confirmation over to them so they could sell them on an alternate website. I told them I needed to think about it.

Amelia and I were livid at this point – we were ready to quit and move on. We started looking for other jobs. Yes, we wanted to have a possibly once-in-a-lifetime experience and go to the Olympics, but it was so much more than that. We were tired of feeling disrespected and taken advantage of. I really needed to sort out what my bottom lines were, where my boundaries lay, what my priorities were and what I needed to gain acceptance around in order to take the next steps.

I called a friend from home and chatted it through with her and, as always, came to the conclusion that I would not have to figure it out or make pros and cons lists as I wanted to, but that I would know in my core what the right thing to do was when it presented itself. It was Friday night and I had the weekend to rest on it anyways.

The next morning, I woke up, rolled out of bed and fell to my knees to pray. This is an important practice for me, and it is the best way I have learned to actively align myself with the universe and my authenticity. I asked for the universe to help direct my thinking for the day and my authenticity to let me know what was up. I asked for a sign. I asked for help in knowing what the right thing to do was. I wanted to go home, I wanted to run, but I asked for a sign.

I needed to write a big chunk of this book that weekend, so I went to a coffee shop early before meeting a friend. There were no seats upstairs where I wanted to sit, so I sat in the front window. I didn't mind too much, because I love people watching and feeling the city's energy pass in front of me.

I was writing away when I felt the presence of some people hovering behind me. I was a bit confused but personal space isn't really a thing in Korea, so I turned back around and kept writing. I noticed through the window that there were some parade floats going by. I soon remembered that this weekend was the Olympic torch relay ceremony. Next thing I knew, the torch was being passed right in front of me!

This was exactly what I needed – the universal reassurance that I was right where I was supposed to be. That everything would work out okay. Why did I take it this way, and not as a cool coincidence? Because I was in alignment that day and was feeling in touch with myself and the universe. I was feeling supported, and my inner guidance was letting me know that things were going to work out, I just needed some sort of external acknowledgment of this. So, I asked and I received. I made no rash decisions about how the week was going to look, or what I was going to say to my boss. Now, I had the validation I needed to be reassured that everything would work out.

I woke up the next morning to a text from my dad; he asked me to give him a call when I was up. All was well, and he had some exciting news. I called him right away, thinking it had something to do with planning my mom's upcoming birthday.

He told me that he wanted to surprise me, but in light of everything going on (and with my mom's strong suggestion), he wanted to let me know that he was coming to visit me in Seoul, and that we would be going to the Olympic bronze medal hockey game! It was also on Saturday, February 24th, but in the evening, so it would work out perfectly. I started crying. It was a once in a lifetime opportunity and I was going to get to spend it with my dad who I had not seen in seven months, my good friend John who was coming with him, and my best friend (Amelia, my roommate, was coming with us, of course).

Practice: Pause and respond rather than react
I didn't make a rash decision based on anger or fear. I was really triggered in this entire experience by a lot of the decisions being made for me. I was feeling out of control of my circumstances,

which is the ultimate form of discomfort for me. I was in so much discomfort and fear. I was in anger and shame. But, I persevered, and continued to make the decision every day to align myself with my authenticity and the universe, over and over, to push the light through the blocks I was experiencing. I woke up every day and chose love over fear. I didn't up and quit, although I wanted to, and I didn't tell my boss where to go. It all worked out the way it was supposed to, because I allowed it to. I trusted the process and I trusted my gut.

Trust can be really difficult for me, particularly because I didn't trust myself for so long. So, to trust now that I am making healthy decisions for myself can be challenging. If I listen to my authentic self, however, I know I am making the right choices and that I am being guided.

If I react, it is from a place of shame or ego. If I pause, I can reflect, regroup and respond in an authentic way. I can respond in a way that ensures I do not owe someone an apology afterwards. I can respond in a way that doesn't leave me feeling sick to my stomach or obsessing over it afterwards. I can be confident in my response, and then release the outcome.

When I respond, therefore, I can know with certainty that I have done what is best for me, as I have spoken my truth. I have set a boundary, or said something of importance to me, or maybe even said nothing at all. However, how the other person reacts is a reflection of their own process and actually has nothing to do with me. People are always going to react, and as I hope I have made clear thus far, we can only be responsible for ourselves. The same way someone triggers me, I trigger someone else. In the same way my reaction to that person usually has nothing to do with them but is actually old conditioning being stirred up in me, the same thing is happening for them. The way I can honour the process in me, I can honour the process in them. This leaves us free of the fear of others' reactions, the way I didn't react when my boss told me I had to cancel my Olympic tickets. I responded appropriately for myself, asking for a few days to think about it. I have no idea what she was saying or thinking about me after I responded in this manner, or over the few days I took to get in touch with my truth and boundaries. If I respond from what is best for me, that is where my power lies, and that is all I can do. I can rest easy at night knowing that I was true to myself.

- *Nine* -

<u>The Fourth Layer:</u>
Defences

Survival mode is supposed to be a phase that helps you save your life.
It is not meant to be how you live.
– Michele Rosenthal

Our defences are a manifestation of all our fears. They are our outer layer of protection. They are our shield, our armour and a way to ensure our vulnerability does not come through. Defences were born, like all layers of the ego, to keep us safe. The problem is that defences linger for much longer than they need to. Eventually, they not only keep the world from seeing who we really are, they actually block us from really knowing ourselves, too. Each defence we have is built from false selves, which are built from shame and shadow. Defences can be a telltale sign that we are in fear rather than authenticity. Use your defences to get curious about what is underneath. Every piece of us, whether it's something we like or don't like, can help teach us how to heal ourselves. Each character flaw or positive trait tells our brain how to think and operate. When we learn about these traits, we can make positive shifts and use them to tell whether we are in alignment or not.

It is a spiritual axiom that every time we are disturbed, no matter what the cause, there is something wrong with us.
– Twelve Steps and Twelve Traditions

Every time we are acting out of our defences, we can use this as a tool to get closer to who we are.

Anger

Anger is our way of protecting our vulnerability. It is the act of choosing fear over choosing love. Anger is a very natural way to defend ourselves, and it can actually make really powerful changes in our lives. I have had to hold on to anger at times to really be able to set boundaries, let go of relationships and move forward and release. Defensive anger is different. Defensive anger isn't about having had enough and setting boundaries, it is about the fear of being seen, fearing that something we want won't happen, or feeling out of control. Bursts of unhealthy, defensive anger will leave us feeling guilty, drained, shamed or inauthentic. Anger can leave us feeling emotionally exhausted and even hungover. It is formed from resentment, fear, shame, the controlling lost self and the wounded child.

Many people are taught that anger is an acceptable and primary emotion, and have acted out of this defence as learned behaviour. Others go the opposite way and learn that anger is a really scary or unwanted emotion, and they push it into their shadow. I didn't realize how much anger I had stored in my shadow and repressed until I really got honest with myself about some of my actions that were manipulative, counter-intuitive and self-deprecating.

Compassion, apology, ownership of our actions and forgiveness are huge ways of moving through anger. If you are feeling an insane amount of anger, it can be a really powerful tool in helping you look inward. What is behind the anger? Anger is actually a secondary emotion, so behind anger will be something else. Sadness, fear, loss and grief could all perpetuate anger. By becoming aware of our anger and what is behind it, we can easily recognize what is being triggered in us. Ask yourself and get curious about what is behind your anger. Forgive yourself for acting out of anger, apologize where necessary and use it as a tool for healing.

Pillar of Strength

This defence mechanism comes from wanting to control people's perceptions of our vulnerability. I am super guilty of this. I pretend I am okay when I am going through something rough so that people don't ask, because I feel I might break down if they do. I pretend I am okay, I am strong and I can get through anything. This can be true sometimes. But, sometimes, I just need a pal to reach out and ask me if I am okay. I am so afraid of being a victim that I pretend I can handle anything and nothing fazes me. I have moved through this defence quite a bit by taking little steps and asking for help when I need it. Vulnerability is a strength in and of itself, not a weakness. It is okay to ask for help. It is okay if you don't feel strong. It is okay if you need to break down. It will lead to a breakthrough.

Projection

Projection is a direct result of a lack of awareness of our thoughts, feelings and behaviour. Projection is making assumptions about someone else's behaviour based on our own beliefs. It is a major source of information for us! Projection can tell us very quickly which parts of ourselves or components of our disowned self we are not aware of. If someone else's gossipy nature is making me angry, it is likely because I don't want to become aware of, or acknowledge, that I gossip, too. If I say something that isn't the sharpest thing I have ever said to a friend, they might not even notice, or make a joke about it. If I hold on to that or get angry at that person, it is likely because of a shame component of not feeling good enough, smart enough or feeling a lack of worthiness. This is a trigger point for us and is a huge entryway. When you notice you are feeling triggered, what is behind it? Get curious about why that person's actions or reactions are really bothering you. There is always something behind it and we can use it as another tool to help us heal.

Numbing Out

We all do it, in some way, shape or form. Numbing out doesn't mean you are in an addiction, but it is so beneficial to become aware of what we use to numb, whether that is work, alcohol, sex, shopping, exercise, judgment – it can be anything. We typically use unhealthy or obsessive behaviours to alter how we feel. Part of the awareness process is becoming honest about what you use to numb out. I like to binge-watch a new show or judge another person to make myself feel a bit better in that moment and forget about my own stuff. Another one I have a hard time letting go of is getting myself so entrenched in drama and other people's chaos that I can avoid my own. This has shifted a lot for me over the past few years, but man, can I still get caught up in it and detach from myself by using this method. I can use food, sex, anything, really, and I need to be honest with myself about when I am using this behaviour in an unhealthy way. So, I ask you, what numbing behaviours are getting in the way of you meeting your authentic self?

Denial

I used to be the Queen of Denial. It is a defence mechanism that still demonstrates if I am in alignment or not, very quickly. Denial is a naturally born defence mechanism that we develop as children to avoid pain. It is a very prevalent defence mechanism when struggling with addiction. If we are afraid something is going to be too painful, why would we want to look at it? The problem with denial is that the reality will eventually always catch up with us.

Using denial as a tool for growth means becoming aware that the denial exists. It is also important to recognize that denial is a basic stage of grief, and sometimes can work to our benefit before we are really ready to process emotions. If denial is followed by rationalizing, that is usually a tell-tale sign that it is coming from an unhealthy place.

Rationalizing

Rationalizing is our way of protecting ourselves from the truth. It entails looking for or claiming a reason for something we don't actually accept to be true. If a guy you like starts dating another girl, you might rationalize that by saying you never really liked him in the first place. It usually occurs through making excuses for behaviour we know or deem to be unacceptable, and this can be our own or somebody else's. If you are a co-dependent (or recovering co-dependent) this will be a big one for you. In my relationship with another addict, it certainly was. I could rationalize anything. His actions, thoughts, feelings – but really, it was all an excuse.

Compartmentalizing

Compartmentalizing allows us to act in ways that we know are not in alignment with who we really are and to disconnect from them. This happens when people cheat, lie or are secretive. If we know that what we are thinking, feeling or doing is not what is right for us, we will block it. Compartmentalizing is a way for us to escape or disconnect. When we act out of our shame or in ways that are misaligned, we need a defence mechanism to allow us not to feel the pain of those actions. The impulses may feel too out of reach to control. This method of control allows us to continue doing what we are doing, even if we don't want to but can't stop. We can then exist in one reality while ignoring the other. Like everything, this catches up with us, and eventually when this defence is lowered, pieces of both worlds will seep into each other. There is only so much we can compartmentalize before it all breaks open.

Get curious:

1. Awareness

The best way to tackle compartmentalizing is to move through awareness of what is behind the actions we are not really in alignment with. If you are doing something that doesn't feel right for you, it is important to look at what needs are being (falsely) met through those actions. Do you have a need for secrecy? Is there something you want to keep separate from the rest of your life? What is behind that? Are you unhappy with current circumstances? Do you feel worthy of being honest or having a fulfilling life or are you filling a shadow need for escape? Get honest with yourself about what is coming up. If you are unsure, ask yourself some of these questions and be patient. Next time the impulse comes up, ask yourself the questions again and see.

2. Acceptance

Accept that everyone has done some things that aren't aligned with who they really are. Part of holistically healing is integrating each part of us, and compartmentalizing keeps those parts separate. Know that you are doing the best you can in every moment and accept that your past behaviour is your past behaviour. You can move forward with new awareness and release!

3. Action

Get honest with yourself next time and try doing the next right thing for yourself. See what happens if you don't give in. Notice the discomfort and know that the discomfort won't kill you. Pick up the phone and be honest with someone else about the urge for secrecy.

Every time you move through the discomfort it will become easier, until it no longer feels uncomfortable, and feels right.

Doing the Opposite

This defence comes from being afraid of our emotions or impulses. If I am really, really angry, I might act really, really happy or kind to the person I am mad at. I am so afraid of how angry I am that if I allow that anger to come through, I am not sure what will happen. The problem is that this defence suppresses our emotions further and leads to holding on to rage and grief, and those emotional blocks will eventually lead to physical blocks.

It is okay to feel anger, sadness, sorrow. It is okay to feel however it is you are feeling. Pretending that you are feeling any other way will perpetuate this cycle and continue the suppression. Moving through this defence comes with becoming aware of how you are really feeling, and becoming aware that you are in this defence in the first place.

If you know you are really angry at your boss but it is inappropriate to act out of anger at that moment, give yourself a pause. Go to the bathroom and regroup. Let yourself know that when you get home tonight, you are going to journal, chat with a friend about it, go for a run or do whatever you do to release the anger in a healthy way. You will acknowledge it, but maybe that moment is just not the right time. By letting yourself know you are going to acknowledge it later, it can be set aside for the time being to come back to, rather than pretending it isn't happening, which is not being true to you. Then, when you have time later, ask yourself what was underneath that reaction. What did that person trigger in you? What fears came up? What old wounds were there? Get curious about what was underneath it. Determine if their behaviour needs further interaction, a conversation with them about what happened, or if the response is yours to release on your own. Give yourself permission to sit in the discomfort of those emotions to get familiar with them. When we get familiar with our unwanted emotions, we release the power they have over us, and we fear them less.

Intellectualizing

One of the most prevalent ego defences is to intellectualize everything. I used to live my life this way. This defence mechanism particularly came up when my ego was being threatened in some way such as by anything it could not comprehend, which were all things spiritual. For example, if you subscribed to a particular religion, I would judge you. I would intellectualize the situation and come to the conclusion that I knew better. That reaching out to something bigger was actually a weakness, because that meant you weren't self-sufficient. I would intellectualize everything (a component of rationalizing as well). I continued my education to fuel this defence mechanism in some ways, to ensure my ego felt safe in an intellectual environment. If I was in law school, I must be smart and if I am smart, then I can handle anything, and things will be okay. If I am in law school, you will believe that I am smart and that I am doing well, and everything is okay. There is nothing wrong with intellect, but the intellectualizing defence mechanism is a block to our truth.

Rather than facing the fact that I had a lot of unknown in my life, which was way too scary to face, I relied solely on the power of my brain. I hid my emotions, I rejected spirituality and I was completely in self. The release of intellectualizing came when I hit my bottom – when I finally had to accept that I just didn't know everything. The best way to move through intellectualizing is to stay teachable. To continuously tell yourself that you might not know everything and that is okay. How boring would life be if we had nothing left to learn?

Taking it Back

Taking it back usually occurs after we have given in to one of our other defences, such as anger. We react to a situation without taking the time to pause and respond appropriately. Taking it back is the defence of that action by trying to make it all better. A friend of mine has this as a go-to defence mechanism. He might react out of anger to a situation (which is really fear-based) and that reaction will trigger a frustration, sadness or hurt in me. When I need to take some space from the situation, he will continuously ask if I am okay, compliment me, make jokes or try his very hardest to smooth it over. If I am not okay, then he has to feel the guilt for how he reacted. Taking it back comes out when we are trying to avoid the shame or guilt that was triggered through the anger reaction. The best way to move through taking it back is to own that you were in your fear, own that you reacted out of anger, and apologize. Apologizing can be really scary if we are not used to it, but it will allow the situation to naturally defuse itself, rather than perpetuating the frustration felt by the recipient of the anger reaction.

Get curious:

1. Awareness
Become aware that you made a mistake, we all do it. Ask yourself what was really underlying the anger reaction and what fear was being triggered.

2. Acceptance

Accept that you made the mistake of reacting and let go of the guilt of making that mistake.

3. Action

Apologize. Be honest and move forward. The other person might still be hurt, but in owning the action that you already took, it will be easier for them to move forward.

Redirection

Redirection is the process of refocusing our energy towards another outlet if we do not want to be feeling or thinking the way we are. For example, if I really want a treat (typically in the form of ice cream) I will go for a walk instead or exercise or eat something healthy. This might seem like a really good solution to an unwanted impulse, but when this defence is lowered, which it inevitably will be at some point, we will give in to that impulse. It might not be the end of the world, but if this impulse is an active drug addiction, giving in to that impulse could mean life or death. So, this defence mechanism can work temporarily, however, it does not get to the root of what the craving actually is. A good way to get curious about redirection is to try to move right into the impulse.

Get curious:

1. Awareness

Here is a little exercise you can do to help release the redirection defence, particularly if you are craving or having an impulse for something that isn't serving you anymore. If you want a cigarette but are trying to quit, you really want that tub of ice cream or to call up your ex, try this:

Put yourself in the position of the item you are craving – whether it be sex, food, a cigarette or a drink, whatever the craving may be. If you were trying to sell yourself *as* that item, so as the cigarette, as the sex, what would you say to sell it to someone? If I am craving a big bowl of pasta, I might say that I am craving warmth, connection, comfort. If I am craving a cigarette, I might try and sell the smoke to myself as a break, some alone time, a time to get outside. Look at what the underlying craving is for.

2. Acceptance

What came up? Do you need energy? Connection? Love? After becoming aware of what the underlying craving is, begin to look at what can be done to relieve that craving in a healthy way. What do you need to accept? Is it unease in a current situation or are you looking for control? Accepting that the impulse is happening after becoming aware of what is underneath the impulse will remove the need to fight it. Know that this too shall pass, and acceptance will give you a moment to pause before acting on the impulse.

3. Action

Make a list of healthy ways you can get those needs met. Maybe calling someone you haven't connected with in a while. Maybe meditating, journaling or praying on the situation will help. Take a healthy step forward in releasing the craving. Know that this too shall pass, and if you do not give in to it but address the undercurrent of the craving, the craving will not last.

Judgment

Judgment is so, so icky and so prevalent for everyone. I judge so often without realizing I am doing it. I judge when I don't feel worthy myself. I judge when something in me is feeling threatened. It might be because I think someone is prettier, smarter or better dressed than I am and that triggers my insecurity, so I pick them apart. It might be because I have done the exact same thing that person just did and it was embarrassing and shameful, so if I judge that person it will make me feel better.

Judging is always from a place of unworthiness. Sometimes, it can appear that someone thinks they are better than everyone else because they are judgmental or critical. However, it is the opposite. They feel the need to push others down in order to make themselves feel better. That's why it is a defence mechanism, because it is built out of our shame, core fears and inherent feelings of unworthiness. When other people judge, it triggers me because I know I do the same. Using judgment as a tool to becoming aware of your core fears is a beautiful way of transforming it from a negative defence to a positive. By simply becoming open to being aware of where our judgments are, I can guarantee that you will start to notice when you are in judgment, and I can guarantee it will happen a lot.

Be open to this being a judgment of yourself, too, because this is where most of us struggle as well. We speak to others and speak of others the way we speak to and think of ourselves. Having compassion for others can help create self-compassion and acceptance. Having compassion for ourselves can help us have compassion for others. The "Just Like Me" tool in Chapter 6 is really beneficial in this area as well.

Gossip

Ugh, gossip. We have all been guilty of it. We all derive some sort of gross pleasure out of putting others down. It comes from our own sense of unworthiness, our own fears and our own need to build ourselves up. It is a defence mechanism to stop others from seeing our vulnerability. Not only is it unhelpful, it can be harmful in some circumstances, too. I've had some major revelations lately around my experiences with gossip and judgment, and have been using them as a tool for healing.

Moving through gossip and judgment

Life will continue to test you. It will test you emotionally, mentally, physically and spiritually. It will test you until you learn what you have to learn from that experience and change the way you respond to it. It will test you to ensure that you grow and become the best version of yourself.

As I've mentioned, I lived with the shame as a child that I was no good, and if you saw me, you wouldn't like me either.

This fear was always present and was first validated for me in Grade 7. I had a great group of friends who I actually felt comfortable and confident with. I was always a people-pleaser and was concerned about what other people thought, but some of these girls had been my friends for years already. I am not sure who started to dislike me first, but it snowballed and in one fell swoop, I was ostracized. A rumour started about me, and then another one, and another one. They were nasty, calling me a slut, a whore. These were rumours that were based on nothing – I was a child, I hadn't even kissed a boy yet. But one of the girls decided that I was her next target and that was that.

That year, everyone gave their friends a wallet-sized copy of their school photo so they could hang it in their locker. A few of the photos I gave to my friends were pasted on to vulgar drawings of me with the word "whore" written on it and posted in school. Two more photos were ripped up and put on the floor in front of my locker. We were hanging out at recess and one of my "best friends" handed out invitations to her birthday to everyone but me, right in front of me. Nobody spoke to me. People would yell things at me as I went down the hall. I felt so terrified, alone, embarrassed and humiliated. The thing is, this just validated how I thought I already knew myself to be. I felt as if people just saw my horrible insides and the jig was up. The fear of judgment, the fear of rejection, the fear of not being enough – they were no longer fears, but what I *knew* to be true.

I became suicidal for the first time at 12 years old. I didn't think I could live through it anymore. I didn't know how to do anything about it, but I experimented taking way too many Advil or Benadryl a few times, which just led to me being really tired at school the next day.

I moved through it, but mostly just because I wasn't the target anymore. A couple of these instances continued during high school, but for the most part, they had chilled out. Gossip, judgment and the cruelty of teenage girls did prevail at times and I was on the receiving end of quite a lot of it.

How did I handle it? Well, I drank, of course. When I was out at parties and drinking, I felt cool. I felt like I didn't want to crawl out of my skin. I could walk up to the boy I liked and kiss him and hey, if he didn't like me, I could blame it on the alcohol. I liked the attention I was getting, I liked being the life of the party, I liked being seemingly careless and free.

Whether it was a boss, a friend, a boyfriend, an acquaintance or a stranger, I cared what everyone thought about me. The problem with that? What people think about me actually has nothing to do with me. Impossible, I know. But, what I know to be absolutely true now is that people's opinions of me are actually none of my business, because they are a reflection of their perception. The same way that if I am judging someone else or being triggered by how someone else looks, what they do or say, or how they react, it is revealing an unhealed part of myself.

The deep need I had for everyone to like me never really left. If I broke up with a boyfriend, my first thought was, "I am never going to be loved." My second thought was, "What are people going to think?"

When I quit drinking, this was something I had to work on immediately. I wasn't going to make it in recovery if I was concerned about people's opinions. I still tried to pretend I could be really fun without drinking, go to parties, play drinking games with water and have a good time the way everyone else was. This faded quickly, as it became dramatically inauthentic and boring. I was worried about what others would think and not about what was true to me. What I also learned in early sobriety was that the only people who were uncomfortable with me not drinking were the people who were insecure about their own unhealthy drinking behaviours. The friends who drank "normally" had zero problems embracing me for who I was, and I will forever be grateful to those friends who showed me so much unconditional love. They saw my authentic self, and never judged me for my struggle. They didn't have unhealed pieces around my addiction, so they were capable of embracing me. What I learned through this was that I am never going to be able to please everyone, and I will kill myself if I tried. It is a huge piece of my people-pleasing sub-personality, a defence mechanism and a deep wound that is taking a long time to heal.

So, I think I have healed this part of me and that I am no longer concerned about what people think. Remember I said life will continue to test you? To ensure you've really healed something?

Flash-forward to 2018 and living in Korea.

As I've mentioned, my work environment could be pretty toxic. There was so much gossip, cruelty and blatant disrespect that occurred amongst the teachers. Hearing my name said in a less-than-loving tone in a language that I didn't understand was enormously triggering for me. Knowing that I was incapable of trusting anybody in the office because whatever I was dealing with would be broadcast and ridiculed, was tough. I had to stick it out for a variety of reasons, mainly because I knew that I was growing so deeply through the process and my intuition was telling me I was right where I needed to be.

Nonetheless, it was extremely challenging for me; this was a test. I was being tested again, as I was as a bullied child, and under very similar circumstances. This was triggering the part of me that feels I am unworthy and unlovable and needs approval to be okay. This time, however, I handled it as an adult, with dignity and grace. I didn't stoop to their level. I didn't take it on. I mean, I had seen them do it to enough other people that I had to know it really had nothing to do with me, right? There are so many examples I can give about the situation and how they reacted and why I believe they reacted that way, but it is not my place to take any sort of look at them, except for to have compassion and love and know that they are on their own journeys. I know now that I am a part of healing old wounds for them, if they are willing to embrace it.

So, how has this shifted for me?

Get curious:

When I heard that some of the teachers were gossiping about me, and it hit me in the gut, I had to get curious about what was behind that. I was feeling a deep rage that wasn't coming from a surface-level anger, it was triggering a very old wound.

1. Awareness

- Journal about what is happening in stream-of-consciousness writing. This means you commit to writing a few pages or writing for a set amount of time, and you just write. Don't write for anybody else or in any formal way. Just write to get it all out of you.

- Meditate on it. Not in a contemplative, over-thinking, what-is-happening way. Meditate in a way that asks your inner healer, higher self or your truth to come out and assist you in becoming aware of what your wounds are surrounding gossip.

2. Acceptance

When those wounds come into your awareness, ask yourself what fears are behind them. Fears, as we have learned, are always behind triggered reactions.

3. Action

Release it. I am all about the ceremonial releasing process. Share it with a friend. Burn your journal entries, find a way to release it and ritualize the release that works for you. However it goes, just make sure you release it.

What are your boundaries moving forward? What are your bottom lines with people? This is so important. It is crucial to know what behaviour we will accept and what behaviour we will not. If you are able to move forward and not have those people/situations/instances affect you anymore, brilliant. If it is something that you cannot accept or live with, that is also wonderful awareness. Become clear on where you need to set boundaries, and then set them.

4. Healing

Respond, don't react. Of course, sometimes situations like this need to be tackled head on. This can *only* be handled in a healthy way if you are healed through it. Take the time you need to feel what you are feeling, let it go and have an appropriate conversation with someone. Setting boundaries is uncomfortable but remember: you deserve to live your best and happiest life. When you set boundaries, you are teaching people how to treat you. Your authentic self can come through when you set boundaries and you can go through the world, walking in who you really are.

It is okay to ask for what you need. If people do not react well, at least you asked. You are keeping your side of the street clean and that is all you can worry about. You can take the appropriate action moving forward if they respond in a way that you cannot accept.

Finally, when you are tested again, remind yourself that you have been through this before, you have shifted and you can handle it.

Always remember:

- Other people's opinions are none of your business. Their judgment has nothing to do with you, as much as your judgment has nothing to do with them.
- You can only control your thoughts, emotions and actions. But, how much power is in that? You have complete control over these three things when you learn what is behind the reactions, thoughts and feelings.
- You are worthy of a beautiful, authentic life.

Ten

The Fifth Layer:
Addiction

The normal question is,
Is this bad enough for me to have to change?
The question we should be asking is,
Is this good enough for me to stay the same?
The real question underneath it all is,
Am I free?
— Laura McKowen

Addiction is the outermost layer of ourselves. It is built on all the other layers, all the suppressed emotion, unhealthy defences and false selves, shame, shadow and fear. At this point, we have disconnected completely from our authentic selves and the addiction has formed. It will run the show. It will take over. It will ultimately maintain the disconnect from who we really are and become a mental, emotional, physical and spiritual disease. Addiction is one of the biggest crises in North America today. As Gabor Mate says, the question is not "Why the addiction?" but "Why the pain?" As we have looked at all the layers and disconnects that have led us to the point of being addicted, it is clear at this point that a complete disconnect from our truth keeps us sick. Addiction is our final way of attempting to meet our needs. It is the way we escape, hide and suppress. It is how we try to feel connected to others. It is how we try to fill a void that has come to be. A void where our lack of self-worth lies. A void where our spirituality needs to be. A void that can only be filled with love, attention and light. A void that is trying to be filled in any way it can be – with drugs, alcohol, sex, gambling, work or exercise.

After looking at all the other layers, how do we know if the addict has really taken form? Addiction is the act of chronically and compulsively numbing out. When we feel the reward of use, whether it is relief, ecstasy, ease, comfort, disconnect, whatever the desired affect may be, we want more of it. The decision to ingest a substance or act in a particular way has been taken out of our hands when we are in active addiction. The addicted individual will continue to use their drug of choice even with severe consequences. If we have come to the point of being in active addiction, we have become so disconnected from our truth that we aren't capable of acting in ways that are really, truly us. We are running solely off ego, fears, reactions and all of the mess.

I've spoken in detail about what hitting my personal bottom looked like. What I know now and do believe with certainty, is that our bottom is simply when we have stopped digging. Our bottoms all look different, and we can recover without hitting the depths of despair. We can raise our bottom and believe that there is a better way of living. Whether you eat too much sugar, are addicted to your relationship, sex, gambling, drugs, alcohol, social media, whatever, I believe transformation and recovery are possible.

It's important to understand further what we are trying to accomplish, subconsciously, with an addiction. Nobody sets out to grow up to destroy their lives, or the lives of everyone who loves them. Everything is so buried. There are four core addictions that the substance or action we are compulsively using is attempting to satisfy.

The Four Underlying Addictions

Security

The addiction to security comes from an inherent lack of self-worth and a scarcity-driven mindset (see Chapter 11). Somewhere along the line, we came to believe that there wasn't enough love to go around, that there wasn't enough success or happiness. That the world was a place of lack and we are not on the receiving end of its graces. We might use an addiction to compulsively feel like we are good enough, to experience security in the love we desire or a sense of safety in our environment. This security instinct is an inherent need in everyone; however, it can become misdirected and seek the external and the material. This need for security will manifest in many outwardly inappropriate harming and detrimental behaviours. We might have felt a lack of security when we were seemingly rejected as children and the shame that built on top of that began to disconnect our authentic security needs. When we are in authenticity, our security need is met. The need for excess comes from the sense of lack.

I needed more alcohol because I was trying to fill a void in me that felt lacking. I needed the confidence that felt instantaneous the moment a glass of wine hit my lips. I needed the sense of belonging I felt from being at a party and the love I felt with the attention I was getting from everyone. None of these cravings ever truly filled that void, and, eventually, alcohol stopped working as the void needed to be filled from within.

Control

Life can give us the dramatic disillusion that we are completely out of control. We are not in control of other people and their actions. We are not in control of what they say to us or what they do. We are not in control of traffic, world hunger, terrorism, our children, our family, our boss and co-workers – we have no control over anything. Except, we do have control over our own processes, our own actions, responses and perceptions. When we become aware of and accept this truth, we realize we are actually in complete control, even if everything seems completely out of control.

The problem is that we all have a need to control the uncontrollable. In childhood, if we are faced with the authenticity vs connection dilemma, we will choose connection. As we have learned, connection without authenticity turns into attachment. Attachments create a disconnect to authenticity and a need to control. This need to control will be pervasive in every layer of ourselves, until it becomes a fear and an unmet need.

An addicted individual will be craving control through their addiction. This might seem counter-intuitive as if you are ingesting high levels of drugs or alcohol, you would be completely losing control, right? However, what is controlled is the pain. The drug helps us numb out and not feel the pain. As it comes up, the controller kicks in and lets us know that it's got us under control – it can fix the pain. That is, until it doesn't work anymore. For me, I was always craving control.

By being drunk, I had a layer of protection. That layer of padding I always craved. I could control your perceptions of me, I could control how I was feeling, and since I always felt out of control of my emotions and thoughts, I could self-sabotage or forget all my worries, whichever I needed to do. It was all about control.

This is still one of my biggest addictions. It is something I have to surrender. Every. Single. Day. If everyone just acted the way I think they should act, everything would be perfect in the world. It is one of my biggest struggles, if not my biggest. My controller sub-personality is a big one for me and can really try and run the show if I don't surrender her on a daily basis.

Control comes up for me in so many different ways. It comes up in my impatience – I get pretty irritable if I am sitting in traffic or there are subway delays, or if the barista is taking forever making my coffee. Why? Because the timing of it is out of my control. The unknown can be a terrifying place if you feel you need to be in control of it. By living authentically, the need for control diminishes. We can trust the timing of our lives, we can learn to trust ourselves and our perceptions and that our thoughts aren't out of control. We can gain control of our own lives by relinquishing control over others.

Sensation

If you are chronically and compulsively acting in a particular way or drinking a bottle of vodka daily or sneaking lines of blow or staying at work until all hours of the night or sleeping with everyone you can, you are benefiting in some way from the sensation of what you are doing. Of course, the high is addictive. The reward system in our brain tells us to keep doing what we are doing, and to keep doing more of it. This need for sensation comes from trying to change the way we feel, because we are not enjoying how we feel without it. If I am in pain, if I am trying to cover up that I feel like I am worthless, if I am trying to escape my reality because escaping it would feel a lot better, of course I am going to prefer the sensation of a drug or alcohol.

As I mentioned when talking about ego, I used to suffer from horrific panic attacks. This particularly took place when I was hungover. At one point, I was drinking "normally" for a university student. This started to shift when my anxiety and panic attacks were becoming completely unmanageable. I remember when my desire to keep the party going and go for mimosas with brunch on a Sunday turned into an absolute need. I remember the moment when I was actually craving a drink – it was the moment I thought I had found the magic elixir to life. I realized that if I just kept drinking, I didn't have to feel hungover. I could party the way all of my friends partied without the debilitating physical and emotional anguish the next day. I could keep my buzz going and still function, without having to spend the day in bed. This began carrying over into weeks, and eventually, I was slightly drunk all of the time. I might not have been obliterated all day long, but I was certainly having a drink before heading to my criminal law classes or to the library to study. This of course, lasted a few months before it got completely out of hand, and the manageability of being a functioning alcoholic was not manageable for me anymore. However, for a period of time, I was able to live in the sensation of bliss and escape and not feel the pain I felt when I put the drink down. When it stopped working, there was the craving to get back to that place. I felt that if I could just find the right balance of drugs and alcohol, I could still find that sweet spot. It was gone. There was no more true escape. The pain and reality and dysfunction eventually caught up. The problem was, I was still craving that initial sensation. I still craved the bliss of the first drink. I believe this is what addicts continue to crave and strive for as long as they are using and will continue to convince themselves that they can attain well after their illness has progressed past that point. I certainly did.

What I had to start doing was to "play the tape to the end." It was a suggestion from my first sponsor and helped when I wanted to drink in early sobriety (see page 89). When I tried to convince myself that one drink wouldn't hurt me, I would play the tape to the end. What actually happens when I pick up that first drink? Well, nothing good. I have no more control. I cannot predict what will happen, who I will hurt and worst of all, I cannot guarantee that I will make it back from another bender. I needed to play the tape to the end as many times as it took to realize that the ability to have just one blissful drink was long, long gone.

Suffering

Eventually, or for some people, initially, comes the addiction to suffering. When my addiction to sensation was waning and seemed unattainable, I became addicted to the suffering. With the pain that was coming up every time I was using, my body became addicted to the stress. Addicted to the adrenaline that was produced with the fears, worry and pain. I believed that I did not deserve happiness and well-being, since I was so disconnected from who I really was, so I became addicted to the misery. I glamorized it by telling myself I was tragic, and that was beautiful. It was an absolute shit-show, is what it was. I didn't believe that I was good enough, and I then lost the ability to see the real beauty in life. If things were going well, I would self-sabotage. I didn't think I deserved happiness, and, actually, I feared it. Suffering came from sensation and control addictions, where if I could control the suffering and it was self-inflicted, when life inevitably "happened to me" I was prepared for it.

FYI: Trying to live a miserable life because it will prepare you for misery to come is just ruining the present moment. This took a lot of understanding and still slips out of my awareness every so often today.

I think on some level, I was always addicted to suffering. I relished tragic stories, watching *The Virgin Suicides* and *Girl, Interrupted* on repeat as a teenager. I fed my pain for so long, rather than healing it. I lived in a state of chaos and drama, perpetuated by my feeling of victimhood and "poor me." Letting this go was not easy. I still slip back into self and into thinking the world is out to get me. I will feed my darkness rather than shining the light on it. That is what my addiction to suffering looked like.

Control, sensation, security and suffering are the addiction's way of living. When we are in authentic connection, it cannot survive. Just as the shadow cannot survive in the dark, we need to bring honesty and light into our awareness, surrounding our addiction in order to release the layer and continue on our journey back to our authentic selves.

There are so many really incredible resources if you are struggling with addiction. The first and most important thing I can say is that you are not alone, and trying to fight addiction alone will be a losing battle. Reach out to someone who has been through what you are going through. Go to a 12-step meeting, get a therapist, talk to someone. When we are in an addiction we have so many layers blocking our authenticity that battling it on our own is too much to handle. The addiction will have been insidiously holding on and infiltrating us for so long that it will weasel its way back in any way it can. This book is an amazing tool, but know it is okay to reach out for help. Your recovery is your journey, and my hope is that by accessing your authentic self, you can access your own tools for healing. I am simply helping to provide you with awareness of your own inner resources. You know what works best for you when you have access to your authenticity. Your authentic self can heal you.

Recovery is hard work. It takes a daily decision to choose love over fear. It is a fight. It is an uphill battle for quite a while. But then, it gets easier. When we move through our blocks, something changes. We access our authentic selves and we can rest a little bit easier. We can gain a little bit of trust. We can have a little bit of confidence in ourselves.

Recovery for me has been the best thing that has ever happened in my life. Regardless of what else happens each and every day, if I stayed sober, it was a better day than it could have been. There is nothing I can do that won't be made a hell of a lot worse by picking up a drink. My life is contingent on my recovery – every area of it. That can sound overwhelming, but it is actually a beautiful knowing now. If I live an authentic life, I can't be drinking. It is not part of my authentic self. It is not what works for me. I am free.

And that's the thing – I have learned to love myself enough that I don't want to put anything harmful into my body. I don't want to destroy myself anymore. I want to nourish myself and continue to live an authentic life. It's not about the alcohol anymore, it's about living life to the fullest.

All of the things that seemed impossible when first getting sober – letting go of friendships that were unhealthy or triggering, leaving law school and changing paths in life – they have all happened effortlessly as I have gone through the process of accessing my authentic self. I struggle with life issues now, not sobriety issues. I can take responsibility for my healing and for my life and empower myself through the decisions I am making. I can look at myself in the mirror now, right in the eyes, and know that there is someone filled with love and worthiness staring back at me. That is worth everything.

Get curious:

1. Awareness

Become aware of the reality of your addictions. We are all addicted to something if we are not living our authentic truth. We might not be living on the streets and addicted to hard drugs, but we could be. We might be exercising compulsively or addictively working. Just because an addiction might be an addiction to work or busy-ness – addictions that are less stigmatized in society – doesn't mean they are good for us. The garbage we feed ourselves that is disguised as food today is something the majority of society is addicted to. We numb out with food in a socially acceptable way. Just because something is socially acceptable doesn't mean it is actually what is best for you. Get honest with yourself about what is working for you. Become aware of how you are actually feeling when you are eating in a particular way, drinking too much or working to the point that you no longer see your family. If in any way these facets of life are hindering you from being happy or living an authentic life, they can be shifted.

Everyone can recover, and everyone can release those vices that we never thought we could live without. If I can quit alcohol, drugs, cigarettes and caffeine (which I relapse in consistently), then anyone can. We will never be able to live in our authenticity if we are relying on the externals to change how we are feeling, acting or thinking.

Become aware and honest about what you are using to numb out. If you have a glaring and life-threatening addiction, it will, of course, be obvious and you might be aware of it already. Then you can move on to acceptance.

The first step in Alcoholics Anonymous is to admit we are powerless. By surrendering and admitting we can no longer control something, we actually gain our power back.

2. Acceptance

Accepting that I had an alcohol addiction was really, really tough for me. I became aware that it was a problem, but actually accepting that truth was another story. I was aware it was ruining my life, but I still had the mild insanity that the next time would be different, that at some point, I could drink normally (whatever that means).

In accepting my addiction, I released the power it had over me. When we accept any situation for exactly how it is in the moment, we let go of control and we can live our lives with more ease and flow. I have to accept that I cannot drink alcohol each and every day. If you accept something, let's remember, it doesn't mean you like it. However, in my experience, when I do accept something, I can learn to see the silver lining.

3. Action

There are so many action steps that can be taken in order to heal an addiction. The first is to surrender. Surrender your addiction, whatever you are addicted to, to the universal energy you have come to believe in throughout this journey. By moving through the steps outlined in this book, you will be able to release the underlying conditioning and reasons for the addiction to have manifested. There are a few more action steps that helped save my life. It is important to note that I could not have done this on my own, and it took support groups, the 12-step fellowship and steps, and therapy to release my addiction. When we are actively in our outermost layer and disconnected, it takes a lot of help to let go.

The next chapter gives you 10 action steps you can take to release your addiction and heal, in addition to what you have already done.

The Design for Living

- Eleven -
Transformation and Healing

Only the truth of who you are, if realized, will set you free.

— Eckhart Tolle

Creating Positive Habits

Quality is not an act, it is a habit.

- Aristotle

Imagine there is a river flowing through your brain, carrying your brain waves. This is the stream you are going down on a daily basis when you are operating under the same patterns, conditioning and behaviours that you always have. So, if I am eating lots of candy, pizza and Kraft dinner and not exercising, I am going steadily down a pretty narrow stream. If I want to make changes to those behaviours, I need to start incorporating new patterns. When I start adding in more exercise, healthy grains and veggies into my diet and routine, I begin shifting this pattern. A break occurs in the stream flowing through your brain, and eventually you find yourself taking the fork in the stream rather than going the same route you always have. There have been many different studies which say that it takes 15, 21, 28, 35 days or so to create a new habit. I am not sure how long it takes, but I would suggest that, like everything else, this is an individualized process and will be different for different people. The important thing to remember is what is coming up. When we go back to the old pattern, especially for days at a time and have a full relapse into our old ways, we jump right back on to that old stream of consciousness, and we pick up right where we left off.

This is why when addicts relapse, they speak about their addiction picking up right where it left off. This is true for breaking any habit and is why it is so important to be consistently vigilant with your daily routine. Daily maintenance helps you to connect with this new you and make a conscious decision to put yourself first every day.

This journey will help you get clear on what parts of your life you would like to begin shifting, and which areas are creating unmanageability in your life. Incorporating these suggestions on a daily basis will help create these new pathways and help maintain the channel to your authentic self you are actively opening up on this journey. I suggest getting a new journal to start this process to keep things separate and new. There is a profound shift that occurs when we see our goals, feelings, thoughts and resolutions on paper in our own handwriting. It makes a huge difference.

Be vigilant with your self-care. Be mindful in your new routines and practice everything you are learning, daily. It will then become habit and transformative.

Releasing Expectations

When you stop expecting people to be perfect, you can like them for who they are.

- *Donald Miller*

How many times have you said to yourself, "I expected more from that person," or someone has said that they expected better from you? When I took a hard look at my life, I realized that a huge amount of resentments came from my expectations of other people. What is one of the best ways you can live in authenticity? Release expectations.

When we expect people to behave in a certain way, we are projecting our own will on to them, without them even knowing. How could this *not* set us up for disappointment? I can do this with my partner, family, friends, co-workers or even strangers.

Some examples of unmet expectations:

- The person we have been on a few dates with goes on a date with someone else.
- My partner and I have had Thai food three Sundays in a row, but he gets pizza on the fourth Sunday. I thought we were having Thai again!
- Your roommate leaves his dishes in the sink.

Now, these things can all be pretty irritating, but there is no need for resentment to build because of them. The best way to handle expectations is communication. Where to start? The difference between expectations and agreements needs to be addressed.

- *The person we have been on a few dates with goes on a date with someone else.* Did you agree not to date other people?

While this could be a total deal-breaker for you, it is important to get clear on where your part is in the situation to prevent it from happening again. Did you let the person know that you thought you were exclusive? If not, it is an expectation, and a conversation needs to be had.

- *My partner and I have had Thai food three Sundays in a row, but he gets pizza on the fourth Sunday. I thought we were having Thai again!* Now, while I was expecting and looking forward to Thai, did I make this clear to my partner? Did he *agree* to have Thai food and make the decision to have pizza on his own, or did we discuss it? If there was no discussion and the ball was in his court to choose, it is a lack of communication, and an agreement needed to be made. This goes for relationships as well. If my girlfriend said she was going to call and then didn't, well, that is a broken agreement, and not an unmet expectation. If my girlfriend calls most mornings, but didn't today, and we never set a time for her to call, then maybe that is an expectation.

- *Your roommate leaves his dishes in the sink.* Have you discussed and agreed upon the dish-cleaning situation in your home? Or, did you just expect him to do the dishes because that is what you would do? It is important to be clear on these issues.

A huge underlying factor in setting agreements can be a fear of confrontation. Because of this fear, I suffered from resentments around expectations for so, so long because I didn't want to have tough conversations. Sometimes, these conversations aren't tough at all but so straightforward and simple that it will seem crazy not to have had them! Sometimes, these conversations can be really tough and bring up lots of fear, shame or guilt, depending on the situation. The best thing is to get clear on what is coming up for you before reaching out to the other person. Sometimes, a conversation might not even need to be had, and once you recognize that it is *your* expectation, and actually not the other person's responsibility, you are free of that burden.

Get curious:

What expectations have you had of others that have led to resentments? Write them down. Be honest with yourself.
Get clear on which expectations can become agreements with conversations. Get clear on which ones you need to let go. Get clear if there are any apologies that you owe because of your own expectation of the other person.

Which expectations are because of old conditioning, and which need to become agreements that will allow you to live in authenticity? Which are authentic needs, and which are based on fear? Get clear again. Write them down. Make apologies where necessary. Own your stuff and release it.
When you are feeling disappointed or angry towards someone, get curious about what is behind it. What were you expecting of them that didn't happen? Bring this new awareness forward in your life.

Letting Go of Resentments

Resentment is like drinking poison and waiting for the other person to die.
– Carrie Fisher

Resentments keep us sick and stuck. They keep us in our victim, in our old stories and our old conditioning. They keep us stuck and don't allow us to move forward in our lives. They take us out of the moment and focus on circumstances that no longer serve us. They block us from being in alignment with our truth.

Resentments, like every other trigger point we have, help us learn more about ourselves. They help us move through more pain, surrender and release. They can help us move closer to ourselves, as long as we are willing to look at them and use them as another tool.

When I got sober, I honestly believed I had no resentments. I was so mad at myself and was taking on the weight of the world as my fault and responsibility. The truth is, there are some things that happened that contributed to me being angry, upset and hurt. However, holding on to these things was an excuse and I had to take my power back by standing in my adult self and healing my life. My perception that I had no resentments shifted as soon as I put pen to paper.

Get curious:

What stories are you holding on to? What pain and anger towards others are you perpetuating?

Write a list of everyone you resent. Write what they did to you, what happened and what it triggered in you. Write down the fears that this resentment triggered. Write down what your part in the situation was. Sometimes, particularly if we were a child when a wrong happened, our part is only that we have held on to it as an adult. Sometimes, that resentment will be us being a people-pleaser and having no boundaries. Sometimes the resentment will be because we said yes to something we needed to say no to. Sometimes it will be allowing a situation or relationship to go on for a lot longer than it should.

In my experience, my resentments are always due to an expectation that was not agreed upon, a lack of boundaries, a fear being triggered or a need not being met. Which one of these is creating your resentment?

Offering Forgiveness

Someone I loved once gave me a box full of darkness. It took me years to understand that this, too, was a gift.
– Mary Oliver

The other person might not always deserve your forgiveness, but you always deserve to let go of your resentment. The anger you are holding on to doesn't hurt that person, it hurts you. Just because you are letting go of a resentment and forgiving someone does not mean that what happened to you was okay. It means you are standing in your power and being free from whatever the situation was. There are some things that have happened to me that I have held on to for a long time. One particular sexual assault when I was 20 years old was a major source of resentment and perpetuated my binge drinking. I didn't forgive that person because he deserved my forgiveness, I forgave him so that I could walk in the world a free woman and gain my power back. I forgave so that I could release myself from being a victim and help others through my struggles.

Sometimes, forgiving means having a conversation with someone. Sometimes, it is actually about apologizing for your part in a situation. Again, this doesn't mean that the person is off the hook, it means you are taking ownership for your role in what happened. Apologizing is a huge piece of forgiveness. The gift of apologizing is that we can walk anywhere in the world and not be afraid to see other people.

When we are in addiction or operating out of a false self or shame, we are inevitably going to engage in behaviours that are not from our authentic selves. I wronged so many people in my addiction, I was so self-centred and really wasn't capable of having real relationships. In that, I owed a lot of apologies. Being in addiction wasn't an excuse, but I had to do everything I could to change my life. In apologizing, whether the person receives it well or not, we are cleaning out our channel to be in alignment. We gain our power back and in that lies freedom.

1. Write a list of the people you owe an apology to.
2. Write a letter to those people you need to forgive that a conversation will be unsafe for, or perhaps the person is not reachable due to distance, death or a lack of safety in you reaching out.
3. Write a response letter from the person to you. Write it as if you are hearing what you need to hear from that person.
4. Burn the letter, burn the list, make your apologies and forgive others.
5. Finally, write a letter to yourself.
6. Forgive yourself for everything you did when you were not standing in your truth. Honour that you were doing the best you could.
7. Now that you know better, you are doing better. You will continue to make mistakes in life. Forgiving yourself is going to be crucial in maintaining authentic alignment.

Embracing Compassion

Our human compassion binds us the one to the other — not in pity or patronizingly, but as human beings who have learned how to turn our common suffering into hope for the future.
— Nelson Mandela

Compassion is a critical component for our own healing, and for allowing others in our life the opportunity to heal and connect with us. Compassion is something that will always be prevalent in life. If we all showed each other and ourselves a bit more loving compassion, life would be so much easier. It is an admirable quality yet seems to be difficult to implement.

As we know by now, when we are judging someone else, it is because we are being triggered ourselves. This comes from a need to feel superior to others or to separate from someone else's suffering. Often, this is due to our underlying feeling of inferiority, and is a defence mechanism to make ourselves feel better. It might also be a disowned part of ourselves, as we are seeing a quality in others that we know we have and do not want to address (the "Just Like Me" exercise on page 81 works well here).

During his workshop entitled, "In the realm of hungry ghosts (attended in May 2017), Dr. Gabor Mate discussed four levels of compassion that resonate deeply with me. This is my interpretation of each:

First: This is ordinary, straight-up human compassion, the emotional awareness that someone else is suffering. I am feeling. It is great to have (and can be lacking in some situations still) but isn't sufficient on its own.

Second: Having a basic understanding of why someone is suffering (this can also be called the compassion of curiosity). I can understand what you are feeling or going through in this moment, possibly because I have already been through it, I have seen someone I love go through it, or I can understand on some level the degree of pain you must be experiencing. It is not to pretend we know what someone is going through when we do not, but to be open to the curiosity of what they are dealing with.

Third: Recognizing that everything that person (whoever we are judging, typically) is experiencing, I have in me as well; it is simply being manifested to greater levels in that person at that moment. It is the most basic part of recognizing that we are both human beings interacting with each other and neither of us is superior or inferior, regardless of the circumstances.

Fourth: The awareness that underneath the person sitting in front of me is their true self. The person I am sitting with (as a friend, therapist, acquaintance or observer) is possibly acting out some pain and trauma which has occurred in their life which is manifesting in some unhealthy behaviours right now. Somewhere behind that is their essence. At the core, we are all divine humans and beautiful souls. It is a result of the world and our development that these unhealthy patterns emerge. This form of compassion is saying, "I see you and your heart, and recognize that the divine in me sees the divine in you." Furthermore, it can bring about hope for people who are struggling, that they are not hopeless or helpless. That everyone is worth loving. That it can be extremely difficult to see the true self under an extreme personality manifestation and can take a lot of work to get through, but it is always possible, and I have hope for you.

This final level of compassion is what we should be striving for – to really see each person in the world as a tiny part of the universe who is acting out of their own shame, defences, addictions or false selves, based on a disconnect from their authenticity.

What is challenging, however, is to have compassion for others when we lack it for ourselves. The main issue with how we treat each other is that we feel immensely inadequate in our own skin. Or, to speak for myself, I can feel immensely inadequate in my own skin and if I am in a place of judgment, it is usually to give me a feeling of being "better than" which really just means I am not feeling worthy or good enough.

We can only meet people as deeply as we have met ourselves. It is also necessary then to let go of judgement of ourselves when we find ourselves judging others. It happens. I do it a thousand times a day even though I am trying to learn alternative thinking patterns. This is one of the first steps for self-compassion.

Get curious:

1. Awareness
I am my own worst critic. Even when I judge someone harshly, I would never say or even think about them the things I think about myself.

2. Acceptance
Becoming curious about my thought patterns and learning to observe them, not attach to them, has been one of the most life-changing things I have experienced. We will cover this in more detail later, but for now, notice what you're thinking, and, *without* judgment, release the thought and choose another, loving thought instead.

3. Action
Use compassion for others to spark self-compassion. Try to make a conscious effort to recognize the pain of others. When a friend is in the depths of addiction, despair, mental illness or any other pain they might be experiencing, say to yourself, "I can't believe how much pain that person must be in to be acting the way they are." When you get mad at someone who makes a mistake driving, say to yourself, "I've done that exact same thing at some point, I'm sure." When someone in front of you at a coffee shop is holding up the line looking for their wallet, respond with a smile and know that you have done the same thing. When you make a mistake, can't find your cell phone or forget your keys, instead of being hard on yourself, calling yourself stupid or useless or whatever negative self-talk you have for yourself (those are my go-

to comments), recognize that we are human and we make mistakes and it is *okay*.

4. Healing

Compassion meditation

Sit in an upright position, feet planted on the floor if you are in a chair or comfortably under you if you are on the floor or on a cushion.

Breathe deeply, in and out, and notice your breath, following it through you, in and out.

Imagine a pink light coming in through the crown of your head and resting at your heart. This light is love, compassion and kindness. Where do you need to send this love? Is it into your heart? Your stomach? Where are you holding fears and stress? Send it to those parts of yourself and encompass yourself with warm, healing, loving energy.

Now, send this love to somebody else who might need some compassion right now. A friend, a relative, someone you barely know. Notice how this feels.

Bring the light back to yourself and know it is always there to be tapped into.

Letting Go of the Shoulds

Sometimes letting go is simply changing the labels you place on an event; looking at the same event with fresh eyes.
– Steve Maraboli

"Should" has to be one of the most dangerous words in the English language. The expectation, negative connotation and inherent unworthiness of the word make it reason enough never to speak it. It indicates criticism, and, typically, criticism of ourselves. But, the emotion behind the "shoulds" is real, and for me, needs to be looked at.

Some "shoulds" I struggle with:

- I should be getting married and having kids… I am 28, after all.
- I should have a concrete plan for the future.
- I should be 10 pounds lighter.
- I should be making a certain amount of money.
- I should know what my life is going to look like.

The thing is, these are societal norms, and actually have nothing to do with me. If those norms align with who you are, that is wonderful. If they don't, that is equally wonderful. I have never been the person who did life as I was supposed to. Let's be honest. I changed courses at university from business – what I thought I should be doing – to environmental studies, which aligned more with me. I went to law school because I thought it was the logical choice, when actually it was so misaligned that I went back to school to do psychotherapy, nutrition and a Master's in health coaching and applied nutrition. Not the norm. I moved to Korea at 27 to teach English and travel Asia. Something that scared the crap out of me because I was so afraid I was too old to be making a move like that. I quit drinking at 24 years old. None of these are "on track." None of these happened in the timeline that society has laid out for us. None of these were really how I figured my life would turn out.

But, all of these positive shifts were shifts into alignment with who I really am. The last few weeks have been challenging for me. I have really had to take a look at what the fears underlying these attachments are. Because that's what they are, they are unhealthy attachments that are inauthentic for me. None of this is to say that someday I don't want those things, but it is to say that I am trying to force myself to be where something external is telling me I need to be in this moment. I am pulling myself out of the present and, in doing so, creating anxiety and tension for myself. I'm actually ruining the beautiful moment and gifts I have in front of me.

It is okay to have desires, goals, aspirations and dreams. It is okay to want to be married and it is okay to not want to have kids. It is okay to want to have kids and not want to be married. It is okay to do whatever the fuck is authentic for you, even if that is not what society deems acceptable or successful. What I want more than anything is to design a life that works for me, not taking into consideration society's expectations.

What I also have to look at is that I am fearing the judgment of others. Nobody specific, just people in general. I am basing inauthentic decisions on the opinions of the world, which, quite frankly, are none of my business anyways. Others' opinions of me are not my concern. And, to be honest, nobody is thinking about me so much that they are forming opinions on whether or not I have kids in my 20s.

I have spoken with so many women who are feeling the same way I am right now that I felt I needed to share this with you. If you're dealing with the "shoulds" you are not alone.

Get curious:

1. Awareness

Notice your self-talk and how you speak to others about yourself or your circumstances. When you are talking to co-workers, are you saying that you "should" be going to the gym but don't really want to? When you are making dinner for yourself, do you say that you "should" be eating more or less? When you are scrolling through Instagram and see a picture of another friend who has recently become engaged, do you have moments of self-doubt? These are all things that happen for me.

What are you being hard on yourself for, right now? Is it your body? Your finances? Your job? Your relationship status?

What fears are underlying those "shoulds"? A fear of unworthiness? A fear of not being loved? A fear of judgment? What is the first thing that comes up when you ask yourself that question? If you don't know, how would you respond if you did know?

2. Acceptance

Be honest with yourself about your "shoulds" and know that you are exactly where you're supposed to be in this moment. If you don't believe that right now, look at something you were struggling with a few years ago, and ask yourself what the lesson behind that struggle might be. Everything is happening the way it is supposed to for your own growth. Be willing to look at your own expectations of yourself.

In accepting what is coming up, it is important to make some priorities for yourself. I have spoken often about priorities and how they are crucial for ensuring what our authentic needs and desires are. Is it a priority for you to get to the gym? Or is it a priority for you to get some extra sleep so you can be fresh for the next day? What is the most loving thing you can do for yourself, in this moment? What will your future self thank you for?

3. Action

Every time you use the word "should," release it. Acknowledge that you are being hard on yourself, do not judge yourself for using the word, and let it go. Replace it with the words "need" and "want" or shift the sentence altogether. If you have just said, "I should go to the gym tonight," change it to "I am going to the gym tonight," or "I am not going to the gym tonight because I need some low-key self-care time." Or, "I am prioritizing going for dinner and connecting with a friend," rather than, "I should be studying and not going out for dinner." The language we use is vital for shifting our thinking and our self-love.

Most importantly, be kind to yourself. You are doing the best you can. You are right where you are supposed to be in this moment. Act out of love for yourself. Everyone's journeys look different, and what a gift that is.

Scarcity Mindset

If you think happiness is a rare bird you won't see much of it.

— *Marty Rubin*

I have spoken about the fear of not *being* enough, but what about not *having* enough? We live in a society where the fear of scarcity is ever-present, so it is only natural for us to have embodied this fear in our lives. How does this fear show up for me?

My first thought in the morning is that I didn't get enough sleep. Scarcity is starting off my day. When I am feeling stressed getting on the subway to go to work, I am being pushed through by people who believe that there won't be enough room for them on the train. If I spend money on a new jacket, I am in fear about not having enough money for that trip I want to take. When I see a beautiful woman walk into a coffee shop, and someone comments on her beauty, I immediately believe that means I am not beautiful, because we can't both be, right? If a student of mine said that they loved Jacob Teacher, I would get jealous, because that meant that they didn't love me, right?

Wrong.

It couldn't be further from the truth. However, this is a scarcity mindset, and one that is clear in every area of society and throughout our lives and our daily processes. The problem? What we focus on, we attract. If we have a negative, scarcity mindset of there not being *enough*, we will either find that lack by searching for it or create it by focusing on it.

A huge reason for this is the conditioning that we have to look externally for validation; we are constantly trying to fill a void with the external. This can actually only be filled internally, but we have been taught that it is appearances, other people's opinions and the stuff we have that matter.

Is that jacket too expensive? Or is buying it simply not a priority right now? Changing to a *priority* mindset and the language we use around money is huge. Money is an exchange of energy, nothing more. It is a currency, because it is the current of energy being exchanged. I have had enormous guilt for being paid for something I am passionate about, but the reality is, I have spent my time with a client, and therefore, that exchange requires monetary reciprocation. This was a huge mindset adjustment for me when first starting out as a therapist and health coach. I felt so guilty for getting paid, but I needed to understand my own worth and the value of the service I was providing.

Do you really want to go on a trip but can't afford it? Write it down and focus your attention on the positive aspects of that trip. How will it feel once you have booked it? Once you get on the beach and relax? These are the intentions behind it, and rather than not being able to afford the trip, with intentions and goals we can make that trip happen, with prioritizing and shifting some mindsets.

So, what do you do to shift the mindset and attract the good? Shift to a mindset of abundance.

Manifesting Abundance

Making a dream into a reality begins with what you have, not with what you are waiting on.
– T.F. Hodge

Abundance is the opposite of scarcity. It is believing that not only is there enough to go around, but we deserve to have it. It means focusing on the good to attract more of that good into our lives. It means changing the way we think and move through the world to attract an infinite amount of positivity. What you appreciate, appreciates. What you focus on expands. It is the law of attraction and it is a powerful tool we can use to authentically live a fulfilling life.

1. What do you have a scarcity mindset towards? Money? Love? Sleep? Health? Get curious about your internal dialogue around these things. Who is that dialogue coming from? Your inner critic? Your father? Or is it a core belief that there just isn't enough to go around.
2. Get grateful. Write down three things you are grateful for, each and every morning. What we focus on multiplies. If we focus on the good, the good will expand.
3. Focus on what you want to manifest. What we focus on expands! If we want to have more positive outcomes, we need to focus on the positive, rather than focusing on the negative. If we focus on what we don't have, that lack will continue to expand.
4. Set your intentions. Let's take a look at how to do that:

Aligning with Synchronicity

Coincidences mean you're on the right path. - Simon Van Booy

You know those moments that seem almost too perfect? The moments that must be a coincidence because there is nothing that could have possibly caused the event? Then again, how could something so profound be a mere coincidence? Those are synchronistic moments, and if you align with them, your life will profoundly change.

I have had too many synchronistic moments to name, but one that always reminds me I was on the right path happened in Toronto. I was heading home from a documentary at the AGO, feeling tired and really wanting to be transported to my bed. It was one of those weeks where everything was super overwhelming and I felt like I wanted to give up. While waiting for my bus, I realized I only had two twoonies (Canadian two-dollar coins for you international pals). So, reluctantly – as I knew I couldn't get away with paying any less – I paid $4 for the bus instead of the $3.25 it actually cost. When I went to sit down, there was 75 cents sitting on my seat. Thank you, universe! I smiled, had a giggle, and felt the sense of guidance and acknowledgment for doing the right thing. It was the "I'm on the right path" moment that I needed at that time.

Carl Jung was the first person to describe synchronicity and to call these synchronistic events "meaningful coincidences," occurring with no causal relationship yet seeming to be meaningfully related.

Continuous creation is to be thought of not only as a series of successive acts of creation, but also as the eternal presence of the one creative act.

– Carl Jung

How I interpret this: Get out of the way and let the universe guide you. We kill ourselves with intellectual pride and overthinking, which really can just get in the way.

My first experience of being open to synchronicity occurred when I was in the process of hitting my bottom, the lowest point I hit before entering my journey into sobriety, and the not-so-coincidental instances which happened to get me to that point.

I heard the people I needed to hear during this time period, and coincidences were happening. I was running into friends I had not seen in years who were sober, and a family friend spoke to me who seemingly told my story. I was on my knees begging for help from a God I wasn't sure I believed in, and moments later, Nahanni, who was 27 years sober, walked by. That moment was no mere coincidence.

Being open to synchronicity and divine guidance has been one of the most beautiful gifts of sobriety. I am now open to receiving the gifts of the universe, and trust that something greater is working in my life, instead of me trying to entirely run the show. I had essentially used up all of my own will, ego and pride, and had nowhere else to look but outside of myself for guidance. Spirituality is where I was guided to.

My view of synchronicity is simple: it is the universe's way of communicating with us, of giving us messages that we are on the right path. Our world is 90% internal and 10% external, meaning that what we perceive is how the world will seem to us. If our internal world is sadness, suffering and control, we will perceive the world to be that kind of place. If we come from a place of gratitude, trust and love, our perception of the world can change. This is to say that our external world is a projection of what we perceive.

We can therefore manifest what we need, intend and perceive through whatever internal dialogue we choose to listen to. I invite you to try and shift your perception to one of love and gratitude, and to be open to how the universe responds. Having just a *little* bit of faith in the universe and your path can help open the door and shift your perception to the beauty that is both outside of ourselves and within. With a little bit of faith, notice how the external world responds to that faith. Be open to meaningful coincidences and get curious about what will happen! I guarantee you will begin to hear the right thing at the right time, have friends call you when you are thinking about them, and cross paths with people you are meant to. Ask and you shall receive.

With the door of faith open to synchronicities, we can transform our belief into unwavering fact, based upon our own experiences. To me, those synchronistic moments are proof that there is something greater than me working in my life. I just needed the door of faith to be open ever so slightly in order to start seeing the magic of the universe at work for the greatest good.

I would not be sober today through my own will and self-knowledge. It was no good to me. I am only able to maintain sobriety because of a daily reprieve that is contingent on my spiritual condition. Addiction is a mental, emotional, physical and spiritual condition, and the way to treat it is to focus on the spiritual. By focusing on that element and using it to shift our mental perceptions, physical and emotional healing will inevitably follow. So have a bit of faith – the universe works in mysterious and beautiful ways.

Being of Service

Find out what breaks your heart and do whatever you can to fix it.
— Abby Wambach

If you have been in active addiction, or really just living an inauthentic life, chances are that you were an extremely self-centred human being for a good chunk of time. I was. And by selfish, I mean that the world revolved around me. It revolved around my pain, my suffering. Even if I was distraught about the suffering of the world, I was still very much in my own pain, in my own crap and not in my truth. Now that I have met my authentic self, I have a duty and responsibility to help others.

This is your responsibility now, too. It is a spiritual principle and one that feeds our souls and helps others transform as well. Sometimes, being of service looks like just being who you really are. It will allow others to feel that they can be who they are, too. By simply being your beautiful, authentic self, you can change the lives of others without even knowing that you are.

Sometimes, being of service means actually going out and volunteering for a cause that is near to you. Help people with what you have learned through your struggles.

That is what I am doing here. I am doing everything I can to help everyone with their struggles. What breaks my heart is when people are suffering from addiction based on pain and not living their authentic lives. What breaks my heart is the suffering in the world that is happening because of a disconnect to ourselves.

Do something for someone else each and every day. Hold the door for people coming out of the subway. Smile at a stranger. Be an ear for a friend. Bring your sick friend soup. Share your wisdom with the world. However it looks for you, just be of use in this world. It needs you.

- *Twelve* -
Living in Authenticity

The privilege of a lifetime is to become who you truly are.
— C.G. Jung

Setting Authentic Intentions

I was never a New Year's resolution person – mostly because I always knew I wouldn't meet the expectations I was setting for myself and then I'd be disappointed, perpetuating my fear of failure, etc. The goals I was setting were never in alignment with me. It was always to lose weight, go to the gym more – the usuals – but I was never looking at the emotional connections behind those goals. That is what intentions are: the feelings behind the goals.

Intention goes hand in hand with desire. Desire is the yearning for something, and intention plants the seed of the yearning. For example, if I am seeking a relationship and I write down that I want a boyfriend and he has to be a specific height and weight, have a specific job and look a certain way, I am not really leaving any room for the universe to kick in and give me what I really need. I am seeking only the external, and not attaching the emotional and spiritual connection to the desire.

If I say that I desire a true partnership with love and respect, honesty and forgiveness, someone who always has my back and I love with my whole heart, now that is a solid intention. It gives room for the universe to work its magic, but also attaches the emotional connection to the desire, thus, the intention is set. It plants the seed.

How to set intentions:

Give yourself some time and space in setting intentions. Let yourself be in a vulnerable enough state to access yourself. Take a few long, deep breaths. Bring yourself to the present moment. Some questions to consider:

- What is your happy place? When are you accessing your most natural and authentic self?

- Where are you? Who are you with? What are you doing?

- How do you feel. Comfortable, safe, open, content, present?

- Now, what do you really, really, really, really, really want? How do you really, really, really, really, really want to feel?

Make a list. Some aspects of life to consider:

- Physical Body: How do you want to feel in your body and how do you want your body to feel?
- Materially: What do you want materially and how will it feel to have those things?
- Emotionally: What do you want to feel?
- Spiritually: What does your practice look like and how do you want it to feel?

- Relationships: What does having a healthy and strong relationship look like? How would you feel if you were in that relationship? What does an ideal partnership look like? What are your bottom lines? What will your other relationships look like?
- Lifestyle: What will your life look like?
- Purpose: What is your purpose in this world? How can you be of service to your fellows? If you don't know, how might it feel if you did?

It might take a while but allow yourself the time to make these lists. It is something you can and need to come back to: they will shift, you will shift, and your intentions will reflect that.

Once you are done, circle 10 of the most important to you. You can take one from every list or take lots more from the list that feels most important for you. Really, whatever feels right.

This is your intention list. Rewrite it. Maybe post it up somewhere. Have it beside your bed or somewhere you will see it. But it needs to be somewhere you will actually look at it, and not see it as part of the furniture, passing it by every day for the next five years.

I encourage you to bring this list out before or after meditation. It can be daily, it can be several times a day, or it could be once a week. Whatever feels the most natural for you. I do not look at mine daily, but at least a few times a week before and after meditation. I have mine printed and stapled into the front of my journal, so that every time I pull it out I can see it. This is what has worked for me.

Practice Affirmations and Mantras

Affirmations are a way of bombarding your brain with positive messaging so you can effectively change the way you think.

I will reiterate: What we focus on, appreciates. What we appreciate, appreciates. This is true whether we are focusing on what we don't want or what we do want, so we might as well focus on the good!

If we tell ourselves we are stupid every day, then our brain will find validation for that. If we tell ourselves we are unlovable every day our brain will find a way to validate that. If we say a trip is going to be awful because the weather is going to be bad or we don't have the things we need and we are not rested, etc., then the trip is going to be awful. Affirmations, along with gratitude and meditation, are a brilliant tool for self-acceptance, self-love and reaching your goals and dreams.

Affirmations can be used alongside every aspect of this book in living an authentic life. Here are a few ways to create some affirmations for yourself if you are unsure where to start:

Get curious:

1. What are you working on right now? Is it setting boundaries? Is it a goal of making a certain amount of money, or getting a promotion? Is it self-love and appreciation for you? Is it worthiness? Is it compassion? Pick something to focus on and appreciate.

2. Add an emotion to how it would *feel* to be in your utopian state of whatever you want to shift. If you really loved yourself, how would that feel? If you made $75,000 more next year, how would that feel? If you were to be accepted to your Master's program, or complete your doctorate degree, how would that feel?

3. Use only "I" statements.

4. Use only positive language. When the unconscious hears the words "no" or "not" it will actually interpret these as the opposite of what you are intending. So, if you tell yourself that you are *not* a failure, your subconscious hears only that you are a failure. Try saying, I am successful and worthy. If you tell yourself that you will *not* eat that piece of cake and bombard yourself with that messaging, your subconscious will actually only hear, "I *will* eat that piece of cake." Instead, shift it to something positive: "I will feel healthy and fulfilled when I reach my target weight," or "I will feel beautiful and sexy when I am eating healthily," or even, "I am worthy and deserving of healthy food."

5. Keep it brief. Keep it focused. Keep it impactful and meaningful.

6. Write it down. Here are some examples of my go-tos and some you can use. I have a ton of mantras listed on my website as well.

- I am ecstatic at finishing my Master's degree.
- I am full of joy and self-worth.
- I am enough.
- I am loved. I feel loving.
- I am light and free at my ideal weight of 130 pounds.
- I am beautiful and worthy of love.
- I am worthy. I am beautiful.

7. After you get clear on what you want to focus on, say it to yourself over and over again. One of the best methods of doing this is by saying your mantra while looking at yourself in the mirror. It is *not* easy, in my experience, to tell myself that I am enough or I am worthy while looking into my eyes, but it has dramatically shifted how I operate in the world. Start

small, set a timer for 20 seconds of this practice every morning and then work your way up to a minute.

8. If you have someone you trust, have them say the mantra to you by using "you" instead of "I." I have done this as well, and it is very uncomfortable at first. My defences were running wild and I kept laughing. I was very emotional the first time, but after doing it for consecutive weeks with a therapist, it felt empowering, and I believed her. Sometimes, if you know you are better at receiving messages from others rather than yourself, this is a great place to start.

We will write our personal manifesto next. Use your mantras within your manifesto in order to remind yourself of who you really are in moments of doubt. They are powerful tools – use them.

Wrap-up: A Personal Manifesto

You have just been through a transformative process and I hope some of it resonated with you. Like I said, trust your instincts on how to follow the program. Incorporate some components into your day-to-day and come back to the rest later.

What is important moving forward is to have your intentions, priorities, goals and dreams brought together. This is going to be your personal manifesto for how you will live your life. You can, of course, change it at any point. Be true to you. It is only for you and nobody else. It will help you be clear on your values and what is most important. It will help you stand in your power and be confident about your needs, desires and boundaries. You can look at your manifesto in the morning, put it up on your fridge or carry it with you. Do what feels best for you. I have a copy of mine that I put in the front of every new journal, in order to look at it when I am about to connect with myself. I look at it often, and it reminds me when I need a kick in the butt or to stand up for myself. It helps me to remain confident in my boundaries and to avoid negotiating or sacrificing my needs, as I still tend to put the needs of others above my own. It helps me be clear on my bottom-lines in my relationships, on what is non-negotiable for me.

You can do this in every area of your life. Keep it broad or focus on one specific area. It is important to tie in how you want to feel in setting these goals and desires. When we connect to our emotions, we can authentically manifest our desires and dreams from a place of faith and worthiness. When we set goals only from our thoughts, they might not be what we really want. The emotional connection ensures our authenticity is guiding the way.

Before embarking on your manifesto, let's do a final meditation together:

A Final Meditation
Pull out your journal or some paper and place it beside you.

Close your eyes and sit comfortably in a chair with your feet on the floor and your back straight. Take a few deep, grounding breaths. Notice your breath and its flow, in and out. Notice how effortless it is. Notice any thoughts coming in, and lightly release them, knowing they will be there after your meditation to come back to.

Take a moment, and picture how your life will look 10 years from now. How do you feel? Who are you with? What would your perfect life look like? Sit with this vision. Gather as much information as you can about it. Go with what comes up. If thoughts of doubt creep in, lightly release them and bring your attention back to the vision.

Now, envision your life five years from now. How does it look? Who are you with? What are you doing? How do you feel, in every area of your life? Take a moment here, and again gather as much information as you can from it.

Envision your life one year from now. How does it look? How do you feel? Gather as much information as you can about it.

Open your eyes. Write as much information as you can about your experience in each of the years we spoke about. Using this information, you can formulate how you will get there, starting with today.

Creating Your Manifesto

Write down a list of how you want to feel: emotionally, mentally, physically, in relationships, in your career, with your health, in every area. Use the intentions guide on page 162 to get clear on what your intentions are. Use your priorities, intentions, boundaries and new awareness to focus in on what is most important to you.

Set some goals. What do you envision for your life? What are your hopes and dreams? Do a meditation that resonated with you through this journey and access your truth. Then, write it down. Stream-of-consciousness writing that just gets it down on paper. Then, get clear. The more visual you can be about your goals, the better. How do you want to feel? Where do you see yourself? Use your intentions and expand upon them.

Set daily goals for your daily reprieve and in the long term.

- Where do you want this true version of yourself to go to?
- How do you want to move through the world?
- Do you want to meditate every day, exercise four times a week or take a vegan cooking class? Include

these in your manifesto by adding an emotion to them. For example: When I have worked out four times a week for the year, I will feel beautiful and my outside will reflect my inside.

Take everything **one day at a time.** One day at a time, you can improve your life. One day at a time, you can move closer to who you really are. One day at a time, anything is possible. Try to let go of the "overwhelm" of a lifetime and focus on the day at hand. How can you be most loving for yourself, just for today?

Design a life you love. Now that you know better, you have the capability to do better. With that comes responsibility. It is time to take responsibility for your actions, and for you alone to manifest your dreams. Think big, dream big. It is impossible to come up with a dream for ourselves that we cannot attain. We are our only limit. Currently, I have designed a life that works for me – not from what anyone else thinks is best or what I think I "should" be doing. In getting clear through this journey, I have been able to create a life that I love. A life that I could only have dreamed of. That's how I know it is possible for you, too.

Remember: this is an extremely personal process. It is your personal manifesto, after all! This is unique to you and, as I hope you know by now, authenticity is the answer. Make a vision board. Start a new journal. Type it up and laminate it. Get creative with how you want your manifesto to look, but make sure you do it. Vision and manifestation are powerful tools and will be the key to transforming your learning into reality.

Congratulations on finishing your journey back to you! I hope you learned something about yourself in the process. It has been an honour and a privilege to guide you, and I hope to meet you on your journey someday. Remember, the world needs you – the real you. By being your authentic self, you will live a life you could only have dreamed of, and you will help others to do the same.

Love and Light,

Danielle xx

Our Deepest Fear

Our deepest fear is not that we are inadequate.
Our deepest fear is that we are powerful beyond measure.
It is our light, not our darkness
That most frightens us.

We ask ourselves
Who am I to be brilliant, gorgeous, talented, fabulous?
Actually, who are you *not* to be?
You are a child of God.

Your playing small
Does not serve the world.
There's nothing enlightened about shrinking
So that other people won't feel insecure around you.

We are all meant to shine,
As children do.
We were born to make manifest
The glory of God that is within us.

It's not just in some of us;
It's in everyone.

And as we let our own light shine,
We unconsciously give other people permission to do the same.
As we're liberated from our own fear,
Our presence automatically liberates others.

– Marianne Williamson

About the Author

Danielle McCarron is an Integrative Nutrition Health Coach and is presently completing her MSc in health coaching and applied nutrition. She is a Spiritual Psychotherapist (qualifying), a motivational speaker, and hosts retreats and workshops to help those seeking transformation in their lives. Danielle works to inspire others to rediscover who they really are and to live an authentic life. She is a recovery advocate and is actively working to shift the stigma of addiction. To hire her to speak, attend a workshop or retreat, to work with Danielle one on one, or to learn more, visit her website: daniellemccarron.com.

Acknowledgments

Thank you to my dear friend and brilliant graphic designer, Frances Martlew, for designing the cover and layout. Thank you to Jenny Papworth and Stephen Petit for editing this book. Thank you to my educators at the Transformational Arts College and the Institute for Integrative Nutrition. Thank you to Shelly and Nahanni, for getting me started on my journey, and Caitlin and Jan who have helped me through so much. Thank you to my family who has always had my back. Thank you to Peter for showing me what perseverance looks like. Thank you to the friends that I trusted in sharing my writing and process with. Thank you to my tribe that supports me endlessly, that have given me permission to embrace my authentic self. You mean everything to me.

Lightning Source UK Ltd.
Milton Keynes UK
UKHW04f1043081018
330182UK00001B/136/P